Windows 10 For Seniors

for dummies

A Wiley Brand

Windows® 10 For Seniors

for dummies®

A Wiley Brand

2nd edition

by Peter Weverka

for dummies®

A Wiley Brand

Windows® 10 For Seniors For Dummies®, 2nd Edition

Published by **John Wiley & Sons, Inc.,** 111 River Street, Hoboken, NJ 07030-5774, www.wiley.com

Copyright © 2016 by John Wiley & Sons, Inc., Hoboken, New Jersey

Media and software compilation copyright © 2016 by John Wiley & Sons, Inc. All rights reserved.

Published simultaneously in Canada

For general information on our other products and services, please contact our Customer Care Department within the U.S. at 877-762-2974, outside the U.S. at 317-572-3993, or fax 317-572-4002. For technical support, please visit https://hub.wiley.com/community/support/dummies.

Wiley publishes in a variety of print and electronic formats and by print-on-demand. Some material included with standard print versions of this book may not be included in e-books or in print-on-demand. If this book refers to media such as a CD or DVD that is not included in the version you purchased, you may download this material at http://booksupport.wiley.com. For more information about Wiley products, visit www.wiley.com.

Library of Congress Control Number: 2016947916

ISBN: 978-1-119-31061-7

ISBN (ePDF): 978-1-119-31063-1; ISBN (ePub): 978-1-119-31062-4

Manufactured in the United States of America

10 9 8 7 6 5 4 3 2 1

Contents at a Glance

Table of Contents

Introduction

Windows 10, Anniversary Edition, is the latest generation of Microsoft's operating system, the master program that makes a computer useful and provides support to other programs, including word processors, photo viewers, and web browsers. Much as an education equips you to read a novel or play a game, Windows 10 equips your computer to perform a wide range of activities. You can use Windows 10 and other software (or *apps*) to read or write a novel, play games or music, and stay in touch with friends and family around the world.

As Windows has evolved over the past 30 years, so have computers — the *hardware.* Today, you can buy a computer as small as a paperback book, and even such a little computer is unimaginably more powerful than (and a fraction of the cost of) computers just 10 years ago. The hardware consists of the screen, as well as optional components such as a keyboard and a mouse.

You don't need much time with a computer to conclude that there has to be an easier way to do things. At times, computers seem overly complex and inscrutable. Have you used a cellphone lately? Or a TV remote control? Why are the controls on every microwave oven different? Why does every new tool offer countless options you don't want that obscure the ones you do want? Well, I don't have the answers to those questions, but I do have step-by-step instructions for many tasks you want to perform using Windows 10.

After many years of working with computers, I find that they reward patience, curiosity, and a little methodical exploration. Seniors, in particular, know that learning never really stops and that learning new things keeps one young, at least figuratively. By the end of this book, you may be a multitasking computerist performing virtual gymnastics with Windows 10. On the other hand, if this book helps you do only one thing — use email, browse the web, or enjoy photos or music — that one useful thing may be all you need.

About This Book

Age is just a number. This book is intended for anyone getting started with Windows 10 who wants step-by-step instructions without a lot of discussion. Numerous figures with notes show you the computer screen as you progress through the steps. Reading this book is like having an experienced friend stand behind you as you use Windows 10 . . . someone who never takes control of the computer away from you.

Windows 10 is a work in progress. Microsoft updates the Windows 10 operating system from time to time to make it more secure and agreeable to the people who use it. (Chapter 3 explains how to check for updates to Windows 10.) Because the operating system is continuously updated, the screen shots you see in this book may not exactly match what you see on your screen.

Conventions Used in This Book

This book uses certain conventions to highlight important information and help you find your way around:

» **Different methods for performing steps:** In general, you can complete a step in three ways. I list the choices as follows:

- **Mouse:** If you have a mouse, follow these instructions.

- **Touchscreen:** You may be able to touch your screen to perform tasks.

- **Keyboard:** Keyboard shortcuts are often the fastest way to do something.

TIP

When you have a choice between these methods, experiment to determine which is easiest for you.

TIP

» **Tip icons:** Point out helpful suggestions related to tasks in the step lists.

» **Bold:** I use bold for figure references and also when you have to type something onscreen using the keyboard.

Many figures have notes or other markings to draw your attention to a specific part of the figure. The text tells you what to look for; the figure notes help you find it.

» **Website addresses:** If you bought an ebook, website address are live links. In the text, website addresses look like this: www.dummies.com. See Chapter 6 for information on browsing the web.

» **Options and buttons:** Although Windows 10 often uses lowercase in options and on buttons, I capitalize the text for emphasis. That way, you can find a button labeled Save Now, even though onscreen it appears as *Save now*.

How to Read This Book

You can work through this book from beginning to end or simply look at the table of contents or index to find the instructions you need to solve a problem or learn a new skill whenever you need it. The steps in each task get you where you want to go quickly, without a lot of technical explanation. In no time, you'll start picking up the skills you need to become a confident Windows 10 user.

Technology always comes with its own terms and concepts, but you don't need to learn another language to use a computer. You don't need any prior experience with computers or Windows. Step-by-step instructions guide you through specific tasks, such as accessing the news or playing a game. These steps provide just the information you need for the task at hand.

Foolish Assumptions

I assume that you have a computer and want clear, brief, step-by-step instructions on getting things done with Windows 10. I assume also that you want to know just what you need to know, just when you need to know it. This isn't Computers 101. This is Practical Windows 10. As an old friend of mine said, "I don't want to make a watch; I just want to know what time it is."

How This Book Is Organized

This book is divided into four parts to help you find what you need. You can read from cover to cover or just jump to the page that interests you.

» **Part 1: Getting to Know Windows 10.** In Chapter 1, you turn on the computer and get comfortable with essential parts of Windows 10, such as the Start screen, as well as how to use a mouse, touchscreen, or keyboard. Explore features of Windows 10 apps in Chapter 2. To customize Windows 10 to work better for you, turn to Chapter 3. In Chapter 4, you create and modify user account settings, such as passwords. Discover the desktop, how to manage windows, and how to customize the desktop in Chapter 5.

» **Part 2: Windows 10 and the Web.** Use the web to stay current and keep in touch. Turn to Chapter 6 to use Edge to browse the web. Send and receive email in Chapter 7. Turn to Chapter 8 to explore a handful of apps that can help you stay in touch with friends and get to know the outside world better.

» **Part 3: Having Fun with Windows 10.** If you haven't been having any fun until now, I've failed you. Expand your tools and toys in Chapter 9 by connecting to Microsoft Store to install new apps. In Chapter 10, you enjoy photos on Windows 10 and put your own photos on the computer. If you want to listen to music and watch a video, see Chapter 11.

» **Part 4: Beyond the Basics.** In Chapter 12, you learn about the care and feeding of Windows 10, which requires a little maintenance now and then. Find out how to connect a printer and other hardware, such as a mouse and a second screen, in Chapter 13. Do you appreciate the saying "a place for everything and everything in its place"? Chapter 14 is where you organize your documents. You back up your files to insure against loss and refresh Windows 10 when it gets cranky, all in Chapter 15.

Beyond the Book

In addition to what you're reading right now, this book comes with a free access-anywhere Cheat Sheet that helps you choose the Windows 10 default application for opening files, manipulate app windows, open a second desktop window, and manage your Windows 10 passwords. To get this Cheat Sheet, simply go to www.dummies.com and search for "Windows 10 For Seniors For Dummies Cheat Sheet" by using the Search Box.

1

Getting Started
with Windows 10

IN THIS PART . . .

Master the basics.

Discover how to handle apps.

Customize Windows 10.

Manage user accounts and passwords.

Personalize the Windows desktop.

Chapter 1

Getting in Touch with Windows 10

Windows 10 is an *operating system* (the master program for any computer). You can use Windows 10 on a wide range of devices, from a smartphone to a big-screen TV/entertainment system: One size fits most. You can not only use the same programs with a range of hardware but also access the documents you create (such as photos and email — files and data, to nerds) from any Windows-based computer, giving you extraordinary freedom of choice and mobility.

Although countless companies create programs you may use, Microsoft attempts to make similar functions consistent across different programs. For example, opening a document or emailing a photo to a friend involves the same steps regardless of the programs you use. You don't have to learn a different way of doing common tasks in each program. This consistency will serve you well when using Windows 10 and other new programs.

In this chapter, you start your computer and work with the *Start screen*, the dashboard for Windows 10. You explore options for using the Start screen with your *hardware* (the computer and related devices). Then you exit Windows 10 and go right back in for more.

The easiest way to get Windows 10 is preinstalled on a new computer. If your current computer runs an older version of (Windows 7, Windows 8, or Windows 8.1), you can upgrade to Windows 10, although older machines may lack newer functions, such as a touchscreen.

Tell Your Computer What to Do

How do you get Windows 10 to do what you want it to do? You can command a computer in many ways, depending on your equipment (hardware). For example, a desktop computer has different options from a handheld phone. You may have any or all of these choices:

» Mouse

» Touchscreen

» Keyboard

Another device for controlling Windows is a touchpad, which is commonly found on a laptop keyboard. You move your finger on the touchpad to move the pointer on the screen.

If you have a computer with more than one of these devices, you might use one device exclusively or, more likely, vary your choice according to the task. Use whichever technique is easiest for you, but don't be afraid to experiment. In the next few sections, you discover the ins and outs of using all these methods of controlling Windows 10. Then you're ready to turn on your computer and use these methods.

In the steps throughout this book, *choose* or *select* refers to using a mouse, the touchscreen, or a physical keyboard. *Drag* refers to using a mouse or a finger.

Move the Mouse

For many years, computers have had a mouse, which is a soapbar-sized device that you move across a desk with your hand. Move the mouse and note how the arrow called a *mouse pointer* moves across the computer screen. A mouse has two or more buttons; some also have a scroll wheel between the buttons.

The following terms describe methods for using a mouse with Windows 10. In each, move the mouse first to position the pointer over a specified item before proceeding:

» **Click:** Move the onscreen arrow-shaped mouse pointer over a specified item and press and release the left mouse button: that's a click (sometimes called a left-click to distinguish it from a right-click).

» **Right-click:** Press and release the right mouse button to display available functions. Note that the word *click* by itself means use the left mouse button.

» **Drag:** Press and hold down the left mouse button, and then move the mouse pointer across the screen. When you want to move an object, you drag it. Release the mouse button to release the object.

TIP

Watch for the word *click* to indicate using a mouse button and *roll* to indicate using the mouse wheel.

Touch the Screen

A *touchscreen*, as the name says, enables you to touch the screen to tell your computer what to do. You typically use one finger or two, although touchscreens may allow you to use all ten digits. In some cases, you can also use a special pen called a *stylus* instead of your finger. Tablet computers and some smartphones have touchscreens. Touchscreens are less common on desktop or laptop computers, but that situation is changing. Not sure what type of screen you have?

When you have Windows 10 running, give the screen a gentle poke with your index finger to see what happens.

The following terms refer to ways you interact with a touchscreen:

» **Tap:** Briefly touch the screen. You *select* an object, such as a button, by tapping it.

» **Drag:** Touch and hold your finger on the screen, then move your finger across the screen. You *move* an object, such as an onscreen playing card, by dragging it.

» **Swipe:** Touch and move your finger more quickly than with drag. You can swipe your finger across the screen from any of the four sides of the screen to display options and commands. You swipe pages to move forward or back. You may see the word *flick* instead of *swipe.* Some people insist that a flick is faster or shorter than a swipe, but let's not get caught up in that.

» **Pinch and unpinch:** Touch a finger and thumb or two fingers on the screen. Move your fingers closer to each other to *pinch* and away from each other to *unpinch.* Generally, a pinch reduces the size of something on the screen or shows more content on the screen. An unpinch (an ugly word) *zooms in,* increasing the size of something onscreen to show more detail.

TIP

Watch for the words *tap*, *swipe*, or *pinch* to indicate using your finger. Touch actions are often called *gestures.*

TIP

See the upcoming section "View the Virtual Keyboard" if your computer doesn't have a physical keyboard, as is often the case with a touchscreen.

Use a Keyboard

A typewriter-like keyboard is a traditional device for controlling a computer and is especially useful when you must enter a lot of text. Special key combinations, called *shortcut keys*, are often the quickest way to do anything (though they require some memorization).

The following keys are particularly noteworthy. No offense intended to fans of keys not noted here. Although you won't use all these keys immediately, you'll find it helpful to locate each one on your keyboard.

Press indicates that you use the keyboard (physical or virtual) for the specified key or sequence of keys (just as *click* indicates a mouse action and *tap* indicates touch). Combinations of keys are not pressed simultaneously. Instead, press and hold the first key in the specified sequence, press the second key, and then release both. (I explain exceptions to this method as necessary.)

>> 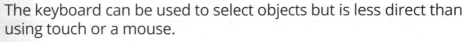: Called the Windows key, this key is usually located on either side of the spacebar, which is the largest key. 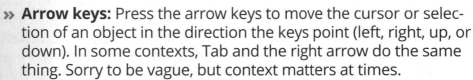 works by itself, as you'll soon see, and also in combination with many other keys. Throughout the book, I specify these combinations where you might use them. There will be a quiz later. (Kidding! No quizzes.)

>> **Tab:** Press the Tab key to highlight an item. Press Tab repeatedly to skip items you don't intend to select.

The keyboard can be used to select objects but is less direct than using touch or a mouse.

>> **Arrow keys:** Press the arrow keys to move the cursor or selection of an object in the direction the keys point (left, right, up, or down). In some contexts, Tab and the right arrow do the same thing. Sorry to be vague, but context matters at times.

>> **Enter:** In most cases, the Enter key on the keyboard chooses a selection, much as clicking or tapping do. However, you may need to use the Tab key or an arrow key to select an item before pressing the Enter key.

>> **Ctrl, Alt,** and **Shift keys:** These keys are used with other keys for commands. For example, press Ctrl+C to copy selected text or an object. (That is, while pressing and holding down the Ctrl key, press the C key — no need to press Shift for an uppercase C. Then release both keys.) The Shift key is used with another key for uppercase.

- » **Backspace:** As you enter text, each press of Backspace erases the character to the left of the cursor.

- » **Delete:** As you enter text, each press of the Delete key erases the character to the right of the cursor. On some keyboards, this key is labeled Del.

- » **Function keys:** All keys function, but Function keys are labeled F1 through F12. You don't use these much in this book, but you should locate them. Laptops often have a separate Function Lock key to turn these keys on or off.

- » **Page keys:** Locate the Home, End, Page Up, and Page Down keys for future reference. Use these to move the screen, a page, or the cursor. (On some keyboards, the Home, End, Page Up, and Page Down keys work as numbers when the Num Lock key is activated.)

View the Virtual Keyboard

Windows 10 can display a virtual keyboard onscreen. This feature is vital for devices that have a touchscreen and no physical keyboard. With a touchscreen, the virtual keyboard appears automatically when the *cursor* (a blinking vertical bar) indicates that you can enter text in a box. If the virtual keyboard doesn't appear automatically, you may also see a separate box floating above or below the text box. Tap that floating box to display the keyboard. To type using the keyboard, simply tap or click a letter, number, or symbol key.

Here are the different types of virtual keyboards:

- » The *standard layout* (also called QWERTY) appears automatically (see **Figure 1-1**). The Enter key changes depending on the context.

- » The *uppercase layout,* shown in **Figure 1-2,** appears when you tap the Shift key on the standard layout.

- » The *numbers and symbols layout,* shown in **Figure 1-3,** appears when you tap the &123 key on the standard layout. Tap the &123 key again to return to the standard layout.

Select Close (or press Esc) to close the keyboard

FIGURE 1-1

FIGURE 1-2

FIGURE 1-3

» The control keys overlay (see **Figure 1-4**) appears on five keys on the standard layout when you tap the Ctrl key. The Ctrl keys are used in common tasks, such as copying (Ctrl+C) or moving (Ctrl+X) selected text. The overlay disappears automatically after you tap one of the control keys (A, Z, X, C, or V).

» The *smiley layout,* shown in **Figure 1-5,** appears when you tap the Smiley Face key. Tap the smiley face key again to return to the standard layout. (Smileys are also called *emoticons* or *emoji.*)

FIGURE 1-4

FIGURE 1-5

But wait! There's more. Tap the keyboard key, which is in the lower-right corner of any layout, to display the four options shown in **Figure 1-6.**

» Tap the Standard button (shown in **Figure 1-6**) to return to the standard layout from the split or handwriting layout. (More on those two layouts next.)

» Tap the Split button to view the *split keyboard layout,* shown in **Figure 1-7.** This layout is handy for typing with your thumbs while holding two sides of a tablet.

» Tap the Handwriting button to view the *handwriting layout,* shown in **Figure 1-8.** This layout enables you to write with a finger or a stylus (a special pen). Printing usually works better than script.

TIP

If your touchscreen doesn't come with a stylus, you can buy one and use it instead of your finger for improved precision.

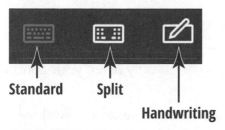

Standard   Split

Handwriting

FIGURE 1-6

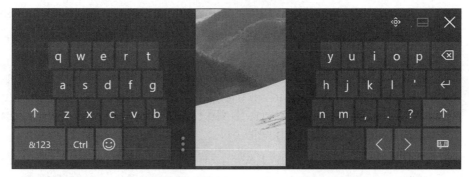

FIGURE 1-7

FIGURE 1-8

Turn On Your Computer

1. Push the power button briefly and release it. Every computer has a power button. (When we can no longer turn them off, the machines win.) If you have a desktop computer tower, the power button is probably on the front of the tower. Otherwise, you might have to feel around the front and sides of the screen or near the hinges of a laptop. Typically, your computer will beep, some buttons will light, and the screen may flash a logo or a message that disappears before you can read it. (Just let that go.) Soon, you will see the first Windows 10 screen.

2. Turn on any separate hardware (such as a monitor, speakers, or a printer).

TIP

The remaining steps in this section occur only when your computer is set up for the first time.

3. The first time you turn on your computer, a series of Windows Setup screens appears. Accept the defaults or change them appropriately and then select the button labeled Next.

4. Select Install Now. (Note the option to Repair Your Computer, used if something goes wrong in the future.) The screen displays *Setup is starting*.

5. If you see a message asking you for a *product key* (a mix of 25 letters and numbers found on the back or bottom of your computer or on related paperwork), type those characters (hyphens are inserted automatically) and then select Next.

TIP

If your computer doesn't have a keyboard, as is the case with many tablet computers, see the preceding section, "View the Virtual Keyboard," for information on how to type onscreen.

6. On the License Terms screen, select the check box next to I Accept the License Terms. Feel free to be the first person ever to read the terms before agreeing to them. (If you refuse to accept the terms, you can't use Windows 10.) Then select the Next button. You may see an indication of the Windows 10 installation progress. Your computer may restart during this process, as well.

7. On the Personalize screen, select a background color for the most common screens. When you make a selection, the screen background changes to reflect your choice. Preview as many choices as you like.

8. In the box under PC Name, type a short, simple name for your computer, but don't use spaces. The name can be based on location (such as *office*) or computer brand (such as *Dell*) or something more creative (*Firefly*, perhaps). This name is visible on a network, if you have one. Select Next.

TIP

You can return to a previous screen (perhaps to confirm or change a selection) by selecting the Back button (an arrow in a circle, near the top-left corner of the screen). The Next button will move you forward again.

9. If a wireless Internet connection is available, you are prompted to select a connection and then enter the network password. For now, select Connect to a Wireless Network Later. See Chapter 4 for information on connecting to a network.

10. On the Settings screen, select the Use Express Settings button for the easiest setup. If you choose the Customize button instead, you'll have to work through several screens of options.

TIP

If this is the first time that Windows 10 has started on your computer, you must create a user account, even if no one else will use the machine. See Chapter 4 for details on creating and changing user accounts.

11. If you have an Internet connection, you see the Sign In to Your PC screen. (If you don't have an Internet connection, skip this step.) If you see the Sign in Without a Microsoft Account option, select it. You see a screen summarizing the differences between a Microsoft account and a local account. Select the Local Account button. (You use a Microsoft account in Chapter 4.)

12. In the User Name box, type a short and simple name. Your user name appears throughout the system, from the login screen to the Start screen to the location containing all your documents. Use a simple, clear name. Your first name is just fine.

13. In the Password box, type a password. A password is an optional security measure. If you enter a password when you create your user account, that password is required each time you start the computer. If someone other than you tries to start your computer, he or she will have to know (or guess) the password to get into your files. (Don't put your password on a note stuck to the computer or nearby.)

TIP

For home computers, passwords may be unnecessary unless you need to keep someone else in the house out of your business. Laptop users should always create a password, however, because it is easy to lose a laptop — don't make it easy for a thief to use your computer.

14. In the Reenter Password box, type the same password again.

15. In the Password Hint box, type a hint to remind yourself — and no one else — what your password is. Do not type the password itself here, or a hint such as *my first name.*

TIP

I use my phone number as the hint. That way, if my computer is lost, someone might see my phone number and contact me. (I'm an optimist.)

16. Select the Finish button. The screen may briefly display *Finalizing your settings.* An animation demonstrates that you can move your mouse to any corner or, if you have a touchscreen, swipe from any edge. That's just the tip of the iceberg. The color of the screen and the text onscreen change a few times to keep you mesmerized as setup finishes. Your PC will be ready in just a moment. Prepare to be awed. Behold, the Windows 10 desktop screen, shown in **Figure 1-9.** (Your screen may look different from the one in this figure and those throughout the book.)

FIGURE 1-9

Check Out the Start Screen

1. Start your computer — if it isn't started already — and sign in to your user account. You'll see the Windows desktop screen.

2. Open the Start screen, as shown in **Figure 1-10.** Use one of these methods to open the Start screen:

- **Mouse:** Click the Start button (you'll find it in the lower-left corner of the screen).

- **Touchscreen:** Tap the Start button.

- **Keyboard:** Press the ⊞ key.

View apps in alphabetical order

FIGURE 1-10

3. Examine the Start screen and note the colorful rectangular icons called *tiles.* These tiles represent available *apps* (short for application programs, an older term for programs or software). By clicking or tapping an app tile, you can open an app. After you start to use the app tiles, they may display changing information, such as the current weather. (See Chapter 2 for information on using individual apps.)

4. Scroll down the names of apps on the left side of the Start screen. You see an alphabetical list of all the apps that are installed on your computer. By clicking or tapping an app in this list, you can open an app. Scroll on the Start screen when you want to open an application but can't find its tile.

TIP Under "Most Used," the Start screen lists apps you recently opened. You can click or tap an app name on the Most Used list to open an app.

TIP While the Start screen is open, you can type the name of an app to open it. For example, to open the Weather app, type **weather.** A panel opens with the names of apps that include the word *weather* (you also see apps from the Microsoft store and web pages with the word *weather*). Select the Weather app listing in the panel to open the Weather app.

5. Scroll through the alphabetical apps list to Windows Administrative Tools, and then click or tap the down-arrow to the right of the name *Windows Administrative Tools*. As shown in **Figure 1-11**, a list of apps appears under the Windows Administrative Tools heading.

Click or tap to see apps

FIGURE 1-11

In the alphabetical apps list, some names are really headings, not apps. The down arrows tell you where the headings are. Click or tap a down arrow to see the list of apps under a heading.

Rather than scroll through the alphabetical list to find an app, you can select a letter in the list and then select a letter in the pop-up list of letters that appears (refer to **Figure 1-11**). For example, to quickly get to the Weather app, select any letter and then select the W on the pop-up list.

6. Notice the buttons in the lower-left corner of the Start screen. From top to bottom, these buttons are your image, File Explorer, Settings, and Power, as shown in **Figure 1-12**.

Rather than buttons, you can see button names on the Start screen (see **Figure 1-12**) by selecting the menu button in the upper-left corner of the Start screen.

Select to view button names

FIGURE 1-12

7. Click or tap your image (or image and name) on the Start screen. As shown in **Figure 1-13**, you see a drop-down menu with commands for changing account settings (see Chapter 3), locking your screen (see "Start Again on the Lock Screen," later in this chapter), and signing out in a favor of another person who shares your computer (see Chapter 4). Who would think that clicking your name would open a drop-down menu?

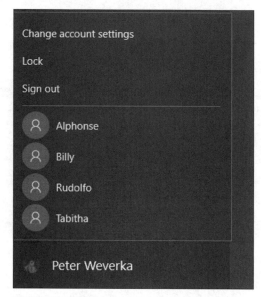

FIGURE 1-13

8. Click or tap the Power on the Start menu. As shown in **Figure 1-14**, you see a pop-up menu with commands for putting your computer to sleep, shutting down your computer, and restarting your computer. Later in this chapter, "Shut Down Your Computer" looks into the options on this pop-up menu.

9. Click or tap the Start button, or press the ⊞ key. Doing any of these actions when the Start screen is open closes the Start screen. You can also close the Start screen by clicking anywhere on the desktop when the Start screen is open.

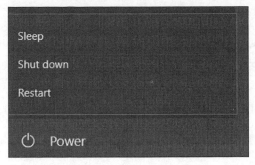

FIGURE 1-14

Shut Down Your Computer

1. When you have finished using your computer for a while, you may want to shut down Windows 10. Begin by displaying the Start screen:

- **Mouse:** Click the Start button.
- **Touchscreen:** Tap the Start button.
- **Keyboard:** Press the ⊞ key.

2. Click or tap Power on the Start menu (see **Figure 1-14**).

3. Available options appear in a pop-up box. Some or all of the following options appear:

- **Shut Down:** This option exits Windows 10 and saves power by turning the computer off. In exiting Windows 10, Shut Down closes any apps that are currently running.

- **Sleep:** This option reduces the computer's power consumption without exiting Windows 10 or closing apps (some computers don't offer this option). As a result, when you wake the computer by moving the mouse or touching the screen or the keyboard, everything is exactly as you left it: apps and documents are open, if they were open before Sleep.

- **Hibernate:** This option combines Sleep and Shut Down. Hibernate records which apps are running but also completely shuts down the computer. When you start the computer, Windows 10 opens all programs you were using, just as Sleep does.

TIP

- Hibernate and Shut Down are equally green options — they save the same amount of power. Sleep is a little less green but saves time if you are returning to the middle of a task.

- **Restart:** Temporarily shuts down Windows 10 and turns it on again. Use Restart when Windows 10 asks you to or when Windows 10 is misbehaving.

TIP

You can also shut down your computer by using the Start button. Move the pointer over the Start button and right-click. A pop-up menu appears. Select Shut Down or Sign Out on the pop-up menu, and then select an option (Sleep, Shut Down, Hibernate, or Restart).

4. Choose Shut Down to turn off the computer.

TIP

On most computers, pressing the power switch also shuts down the computer. On a laptop, closing the lid may shut down the laptop or put it in sleep or hibernation mode.

TIP

For a desktop computer, consider using a power strip to plug in the computer, the monitor, and the printer. After you shut down or hibernate the computer, turn off the power strip to save power.

Start Again on the Lock Screen

1. Turn on your computer. Every time you turn on your computer, the Lock screen appears. As shown in **Figure 1-15**, the Lock screen displays the time, day, and date along with a photo. (You discover how to change this photo in Chapter 3.)

2. Dismiss the Lock screen with one of these methods:

- **Mouse:** Click anywhere, roll the wheel toward you, or drag the entire screen up.

- **Touchscreen:** Drag the entire screen up.

- **Keyboard:** Press any key.

FIGURE 1-15

3. If you don't use a password, wait briefly for the Start screen to appear. If you use a password, enter it with a physical or virtual keyboard. Then press Enter or select the arrow next to the password box to display the Windows desktop screen.

4. Take a break before reading Chapter 2.

Chapter 2
Using the Start Screen and Apps

The Windows 10 *Start screen* appears when you select the Start button in the lower-left corner of the screen or you press the ⊞ key. It provides access to just about everything you do with Windows 10.

The Start screen is home to numerous programs, or *apps* (short for applications). An app performs a function or displays information. For example, the Weather app offers weather reports (surprise!) and the Money app lets you track stocks and bonds. Apps can be simple or complex.

Apps appear on the Start screen as *tiles*. A tile, which may be square or rectangular, displays the app's name and symbol or icon. A tile that displays changing information is called a *live tile*. An open app typically covers the screen, hiding other apps that are open. However, some apps can be displayed side-by-side with a function called *snap*.

Two categories of apps are available:

» *Windows 10 apps* are modern looking and rich with information. They are designed to work with touchscreens as well as with a mouse. Weather and Money are the first two such apps you use in this chapter. (The News and Sports apps function similarly to the Money app, each with a unique focus.)

» *Desktop apps* always open with the desktop behind them. Most desktop apps don't have the look or consistent functions of Windows 10 apps. Desktop apps may not respond to touch as reliably as Windows 10 apps.

You select an app to use in one of two ways:

» **Mouse:** Move the mouse pointer over an app tile. Click the left mouse button to select the tile and open the app.

» **Touchscreen:** Tap the app tile with one of your fingers.

In this chapter, you open, close, and use some of the apps that come with Windows 10. You also switch between apps and the Start screen, and switch directly between two apps. You find out how to search for apps not shown on the Start screen. You discover how to organize the Start screen by rearranging tiles into groups. Finally, you can try out Cortana, the robotic Windows digital assistant.

See Chapter 9 for information on getting new apps from the Windows Store.

 TIP

Although some steps are specific to one app, most of the steps you follow in this chapter can be repeated in any app.

Open the Weather and Money Apps

1. Select the Start button, as shown in **Figure 2-1**. Selecting this button opens the Start screen, also shown in **Figure 2-1**.

   You can also open the Start screen by pressing the ⊞ key.

Weather tile

FIGURE 2-1

2. Use the mouse or a finger to select the tile labeled Weather. The Weather app opens, as shown in **Figure 2-2**. It shows the current temperature and weather forecast for your default location. Select the Show Options button (see **Figure 2-2**). As do most apps, Weather has a Show Options button in the upper-left corner. Select this button to expand the app bar and see the names of options on the app bar. Select the button again to collapse options on the app bar.

TIP

The first time you open the Weather app, a Welcome screen appears. It asks whether you want to show temperatures in Fahrenheit or Celsius and what your default location is. By default location, the Weather app wants to know where you live, or, if you're a vagabond, where you spend the majority of your time. Enter a city or town name in the Search box, and from the menu that appears as you type, select the name of the town or city that you call home. You can always change these settings by selecting the Settings button in the app bar and choosing options on the Settings screen. (See "Change App Settings," later in this chapter.)

Show Options button

FIGURE 2-2

3. Switch back to the Start screen using one of these methods:

- Tap or click the Start button.

- Press the ⊞ key.

TIP

Focus on the method you think is easiest. However, keep in mind that alternative methods of controlling your computer are always available.

4. On the Start screen, check to see whether the Weather tile is displaying current weather information, as in **Figure 2-3**. The Weather app has a *live tile.* As with the News app and the Money app, the Weather tile app on the Start screen displays changing information.

Weather has a live tile

FIGURE 2-3

5. Switch back to the Weather app by selecting its tile with the mouse or your finger. The Weather app reappears.

6. Switch back to the Start screen.

7. Select the Money tile (look for a green icon). The Money home screen appears, as shown in **Figure 2-4.**

If the Money tile doesn't appear on your Start screen, scroll in the alphabetical list of apps to the Money app tile and select it.

TIP

8. Scroll downward for an overview of the Money app, which offers market reports and financial news. Use these techniques to scroll:

- **Mouse:** Drag the scroll box on the right side of the screen up or down. If your mouse has a wheel, you can also turn the mouse wheel to scroll.

- **Touchscreen:** Swipe the screen up or down.

9. Switch to the Start screen by selecting the Windows button or pressing the ⊞ key. Note that the live Money tile (if it appears on your Start screen) shows financial data.

FIGURE 2-4

10. On the Start screen, select the Weather tile. Switch back and forth between the Weather app and the Start screen a few times to get comfortable with switching between an app and the Start screen.

Switch among Open Apps

1. Open the Weather app, as in the preceding section.

2. Switch to the Start screen and open the Money app.

3. Switch to Task view, as shown in **Figure 2-5.** In Task view, thumbnail versions of all open apps appear on the screen. You can switch to Task view with one of these methods:

   - **Mouse:** Click the Task View button on the taskbar (refer to **Figure 2-5**).

   - **Touchscreen:** Swipe from the left edge of the screen or tap the Task View button.

   - **Keyboard:** Press ⊞+Tab.

Task View button   **Select an icon to switch apps**

FIGURE 2-5

4. Select the Weather app to switch to it. Task view offers one way of switching between apps. Use the Task View method to switch between apps when many apps are open onscreen. Seeing tiles for all open apps makes switching from one app to another easy.

TIP

Chapter 5 explains how you can open a second desktop on the screen and in so doing keep some of your open apps on one screen and some of your open apps on another. When you're running many apps, opening a second desktop is a great way to be able to switch quickly from one app to another.

5. Select the Money app icon on the taskbar to switch to the Money app (refer to **Figure 2-5**). The taskbar is located along the bottom of the screen. Whenever you open an app, Windows 10 places its icon on the taskbar. You can select an icon on the taskbar to switch to an open app.

TIP

Some icons appear permanently on the taskbar. For example, the File Explorer icon is always on the taskbar regardless of whether File Explorer is running. Chapter 5 explains how you can pin your favorite apps to the taskbar. Pinning an app to the taskbar places an icon there so that you can open an app quickly.

6. Press Alt+Tab and continue to hold down the Alt key after you press Tab. A window showing thumbnails of all open apps appears onscreen, as shown in **Figure 2-6**. While holding down the Alt key, press the left- or right-arrow key to select the Weather thumbnail, and then release the Alt key. The Weather app appears onscreen. Pressing Alt+Tab is yet another way to switch between open applications.

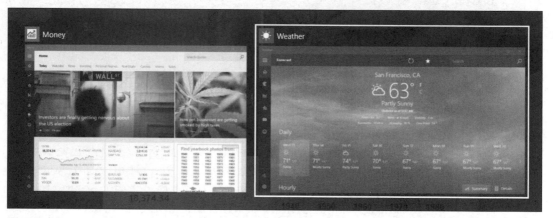

FIGURE 2-6

TIP

Chapter 5 demonstrates techniques for moving windows onscreen, changing the size of windows, and snapping windows to the side of the screen.

Close the Weather and Money Apps

1. On the Start screen, select the Weather app if the Weather app isn't already open.

2. Close the Weather app (any open app) with one of these methods:

- **Mouse:** Click the Close button (the X) in the upper-right corner of the screen.

- **Touchscreen:** Tap the Close button (the X) in the upper-right corner of the screen.

- **Keyboard:** Press Alt+F4.

TIP

You don't have to close apps. However, having unneeded apps open makes switching between apps more of a challenge because of unneeded thumbnails in the app switcher.

3. On the Start screen again, select the Weather app tile to reopen the Weather App. Notice the Weather app icon on the taskbar along the bottom of the screen.

4. Display the context menu on the Weather app icon and choose Close Window on the context menu, as shown in **Figure 2-7.** Use one of these techniques to display the context menu on a taskbar icon:

- **Mouse:** Right-click the icon.

- **Touchscreen:** Touch and hold the icon until a rectangle appears around the icon, and then release your finger.

You can close an app from the taskbar

FIGURE 2-7

TIP

To close an app that is frozen (an app that is unresponsive), press Ctrl+Shift+Esc. The Task Manager opens. It lists all apps that are currently running. Select the app you want to close and then select the End Task button.

Use the App Bar

1. From the Start screen, open the Money app.

2. The *app bar* contains functions specific to the current app. Display the app bar by selecting the Show Options button. **Figure 2-8** shows the app bar in the Money app.

Show Options button

App bar

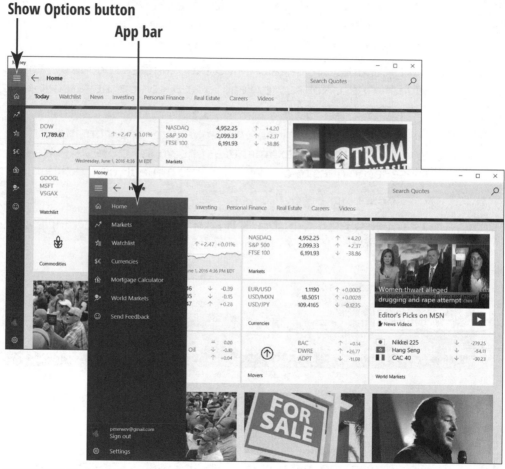

FIGURE 2-8

TIP

The app bar may appear across the top of the screen, the left side of the screen, or in both locations.

3. In the Money app, the app bar leads you to different functions. Select Markets, for example, to see how different markets (DOW, NASDAQ, and others) are performing.

4. Display the app bar in Money again. Then select the Mortgage Calculator button. A screen appears to help you determine how much money you can borrow and what your monthly payment on different loans will be.

5. Display the app bar again and take notice of the Home button. Wherever you travel in an app, you can return to the app *home screen* by selecting this button.

In most apps, you can select the Back button (a left-pointing arrow) to return to the previous screen you viewed. The Back button is found in the upper-left corner of most screens.

Add a Location in Weather

1. From the Start screen, open the Weather app if it isn't already open. With the Weather app on the screen, select the Show Options button to expand the app bar and see the option names. As shown in **Figure 2-9**, the Weather app bar appears on the left side of the screen.

2. Select the Favorites button on the app bar. The Favorites screen appears, as shown in **Figure 2-10**. Your screen will show a different live tile.

3. Select the Add Favorite Places tile, which looks like a plus in a square. The Add to Favorites screen appears.

4. Type a location name, such as a city, in the box under Add to Favorites, as shown in **Figure 2-11**. As you type, matching location names appear below the box. If you see the location you want, select that name to add a tile for that location to the Places screen. No need to click the Add button, unless your location does not appear automatically.

You can add other locations by repeating Steps 3 and 4.

5. Select the tile for the location you added. The Weather app displays full information for the location you selected.

App bar

FIGURE 2-9

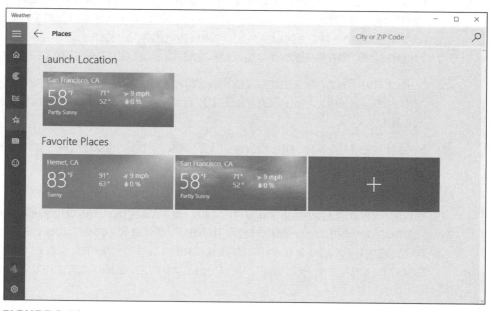

FIGURE 2-10

Type in the box

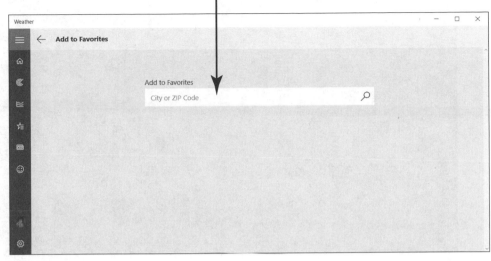

FIGURE 2-11

TIP

You can switch among multiple locations by using the Favorites button on the app bar.

6. Return to the Start screen. Your new favorite location does not appear on the Weather tile — yet. Select the Weather tile to return to the weather app. You see your new favorite location, as shown in **Figure 2-12**. In addition to the app bar on the left side of the screen, an app bar for the selected location appears along the top of the screen.

7. Select the Pin button at the top of the screen (refer to **Figure 2-12**). Selecting this button adds a tile for the current location to the Start screen. (If you don't see the Pin button, repeat Steps 2–5 to add a favorite location.)

8. Return to the Start screen. The original Weather tile appears, as well as the new tile. You may have to scroll downward to see the new Weather tile.

9. Select the new Weather tile to open the app with that location.

10. Display the app bar for Weather, which is shown in **Figure 2-13.** Select the Unpin button at the top of the screen to remove the tile for the current location from the Start screen. If the Unpin button doesn't appear, repeat Step 7.

Pin this location to the Weather app tile on the Start screen

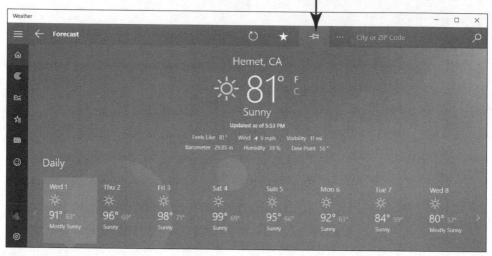

FIGURE 2-12

Select Unpin

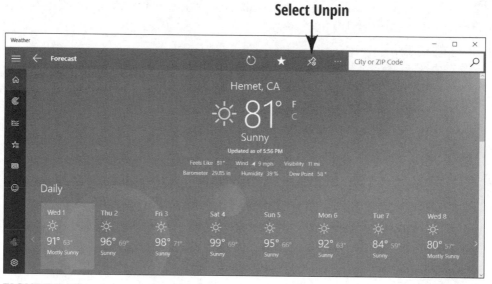

FIGURE 2-13

Return to the Start screen. The location you unpinned no longer appears.

TIP

Add locations for friends, family, and travel destinations and pin these new locations to the Start screen. See the section "Arrange and Group Apps on the Start Screen," later in this chapter, if you want to group these tiles.

Change App Settings

1. On the Start screen, select the Weather tile if the Weather app isn't open already.

2. In the Weather app, select the Settings button on the app bar. The Settings screen appears, as shown in **Figure 2-14**. Settings is the last option. If you have trouble locating it, select the Show Options button, the topmost button the app bar, to see the buttons on the app bar.

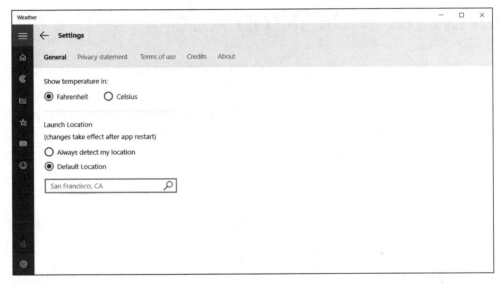

FIGURE 2-14

TIP

It may be hard to remember whether you need the Settings panel or the app bar to do something. In general, functions on the app bar are used more frequently than those on the Settings panel. When in doubt, guess — that's how discoveries are made.

3. Choose whether to show air temperatures in Fahrenheit or Celsius.

4. Choose a Launch Location option. The Always Detect My Location option tells the Weather app to note by way of your Internet connection where you are currently and give the weather report for that place. Select Default Location and enter the name of the place where you live if you want to receive weather forecasts for that place.

TIP

Select Privacy Statement in the Settings window if you're interested in how Microsoft collects data about you when you use Weather and other apps made by Microsoft. Your browser opens to a web page clotted with legalese and other obfuscations. You may have noticed that ads appear in the Weather app. Starting on this web page, you can keep the ads from displaying by opting out of ads.

TIP

Changes to settings take effect immediately. You don't have to save or activate your changes.

Search for a Desktop App

1. Open the Start screen: Click the Windows button in the lower-left corner of the desktop or press ⊞.

2. In the Search the Web and Windows box (you find it to the right of the Windows button), type **calc** (the first four letters of the word *calculator*). The Search panel appears on the left side of the screen, as shown in **Figure 2-15**. The Search panel lists app names, program names, settings, files, and web pages with the term you entered. You can search for just about anything from the Search the Web and Windows box.

TIP

Select an icon at the bottom of the Search panel (refer to **Figure 2-15**) to narrow your search. For example, select the Settings icon to look for a customization command; select Music to search for a music file; or select Web to narrow your search to things on the Internet.

3. Type **ulator** to finish typing the word *calculator.* The Search panel lists only items with the complete word *calculator* in them, including the Calculator app.

4. Select the Calculator app to open it on the desktop, as shown in **Figure 2-16**. To perform a calculation, select the buttons on the screen or use a keyboard.

5. Return to the Start screen: Click the Windows button in the lower-left corner of the desktop or press ⊞.

6. Type **calculator** again in the Search the Web and Windows box. Again, the Search panel appears, and the Calculator app appears at the top of the Search panel (refer to **Figure 2-16**).

Narrow your search

Search text

FIGURE 2-15

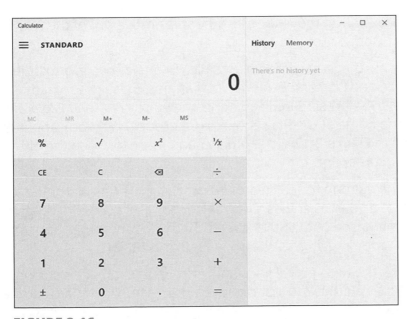

FIGURE 2-16

7. Display the context menu on the Calculator app and choose Pin to Start on the context menu. (If Unpin from Start appears on the context menu, the Calculator tile is already on the Start screen; disregard this step.) Use one of these techniques to display the context menu:

- **Mouse:** Right-click Calculator in the Search panel.
- **Touchscreen:** Touch and hold Calculator in the Search panel until the context menu appears, and then release your finger.

8. Open the Start screen and note where the Calculator tile appears. You can open the Calculator by selecting this tile.

TIP

To remove a tile from the Start screen, display its context menu and select Unpin from Start.

Arrange and Group Apps on the Start Screen

1. You can rearrange tiles on the Start screen by dragging them to different places. On the Start screen, drag the Calculator tile to a different location. As you move the tile, other tiles move out of the way, like a game of Dodge Tile.

2. To start with, the Start screen places tiles in one of two groups: Life at a Glance and Play and Explore. You can find these group names at the top of the start screen. Tap or click the words *Play and Explore* to change the name of the Play and Explore group. A text box appears, as shown in **Figure 2-17**. Enter a new name here (or keep the old name) and press Enter.

3. Create a new group for Calculator by dragging the Calculator tile to the right of all the other tiles. Drag Calculator as if you were dragging it off the right side of the Start screen. Two horizontal lines appear after you stop dragging, as shown in **Figure 2-18, left**.

4. Tap or click the two vertical lines and you see a text box, as shown in **Figure 2-18, middle**. You just created a new group with Calculator as the only tile.

Click or tap to change a group name

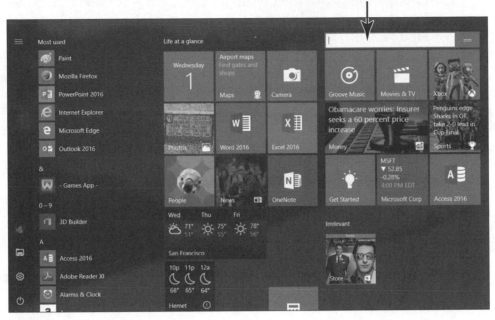

FIGURE 2-17

Tap or click to display the text box

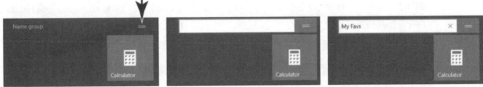

FIGURE 2-18

5. Type a name for the group into the text box, as shown in **Figure 2-18, right**. You can change the name at any time by repeating Steps 3 and 4. To remove the name, select the X to the right of the text box. Create groups to organize app tiles on the Start screen.

6. Use one of the following methods to open the context menu on the Calculator tile:

- **Mouse:** Position the pointer over the tile and right-click. (A left click would open the app.)

- **Touchscreen:** Swipe slightly down or up on the tile. (A direct tap would open the app.)

Change the size of the Calculator tile. On the context menu, select Resize and then select the Wide option on the submenu, as shown in **Figure 2-19**. (The options you see on a touchscreen are the same, but are arranged differently on the context menu.) As well as the Wide, Medium, and Small options, Windows 10 provides a Large option for some tiles.

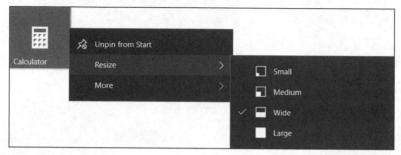

FIGURE 2-19

Choose the Large or Wide resize option for apps you use often. The larger the tile, the easier it is to find on the Start screen.

7. Locate a tile on the Start screen that doesn't need to be there. Then select the tile and select Unpin from Start on the context menu to remove the tile from the Start screen. (See Step 6 if you need instructions for displaying the context menu.)

The Start screen becomes more useful and personal when you eliminate tiles that you don't need and arrange tiles to suit your sense of order.

Ask Questions of Cortana

1. Click or tap in the box on the left side of the taskbar. As soon as you click or tap, a "digital assistant" called Cortana springs to life, as shown in **Figure 2-20, left**. Cortana can respond to questions you ask with your voice.

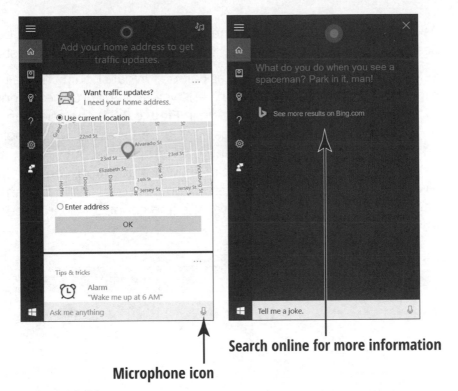

Microphone icon

Search online for more information

FIGURE 2-20

TIP

To start using Cortana for the first time, select the I'm In! button, read the privacy statement that appears, and select the I Agree button (or select No Thanks if you change your mind about using Cortana). Then follow the onscreen instructions for setting up Cortana.

TIP

To use Cortana, your computer's microphone must be up and running. Turn to Chapter 13 if the microphone on your computer isn't connected or working properly.

2. Select the Microphone icon and say aloud, "Tell me a joke." As you say these words, they appear in the text box, and if all goes right, Cortana recites a joke. As well, the words of the joke appear on the screen, as shown in **Figure 2-20, right**.

3. Say the words "Hey, Cortana" and then ask, "What is the weather in Chicago, Illinois?" Instead of selecting the Microphone icon to alert Cortana that you want to ask a question, you can say the words "Hey, Cortana." Cortana gives you the weather in Chicago.

TIP

Ask questions of Cortana while the word *Listening* appears in the box. Seeing this word tells you that Cortana is prepared to field a question.

4. Select the Microphone icon and ask aloud, "What should I name my cat?" In this instance, Cortana can't answer, so your browser opens to the Bing search engine, as shown in **Figure 2-21**. The question "What should I name my cat?" has been entered in the Search box, and the results of the search point to information about cat names. Regardless of whether Cortana can answer a question, you can always select the Search More Results on Bing.com link in Cortana to open your browser to the Bing website and conduct a search there (refer to **Figure 2-20, right**).

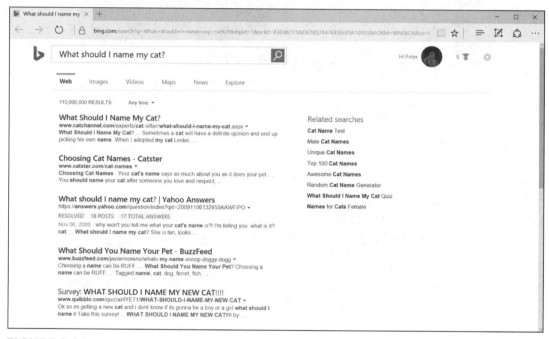

FIGURE 2-21

5. Return to Cortana and scroll down the screen by dragging the scrollbar or swiping downward. On the basis of questions you've asked, Cortana provides newspaper articles and other information that it thinks are of interest to you. You can click or tap an article to open it on your browser.

6. Cortana can remind you to attend events and appointments. Say the words "Hey, Cortana" and then say, "Remind me to walk the dog in one hour." As shown in **Figure 2-22, left**, Cortana presents a reminder screen. As long as you begin by saying "Remind me," Cortana can record reminders like this. Say "Yes" or select the Remind button.

7. On the Cortana App bar, select the Reminders button (the light bulb) to go to the Reminders screen, as shown in **Figure 2-22, right.** You see the reminder to walk the dog.

Say "Remind me" to record a reminder

Go to the Reminders screen

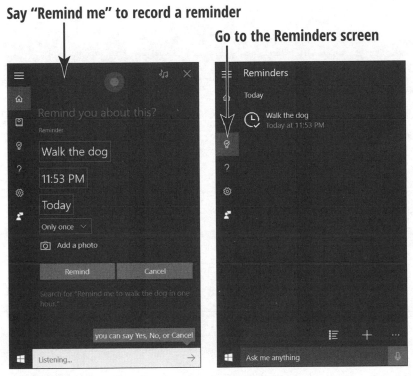

FIGURE 2-22

Chapter 3
Adjusting Windows 10 Settings

O ut of the box, Windows 10 is showy and colorful. If you don't like that look, however, you can change the photos and colors you see on the screen. Adjusting Windows 10 settings can also make Windows 10 easier and more fun to use. When you're ready, you can dive in and make Windows 10 yours.

In this chapter, you personalize the Lock screen. You see this screen many times a day, so it should please you. You also choose a picture to identify your account on the Start menu. This chapter also explains how to make your screen easier to see and enable features such as Narrator, which reads aloud content from the screen. Finally, you discover how to customize the Start menu.

Many people leave Windows 10 largely as they found it. Some love to tweak, tinker, and tune. How far you go in personalizing Windows 10 is up to you — it's your computer, after all.

 See Chapter 4 for information on changing passwords and other User settings.

TIP

Access the Settings Screen

TIP

1. Starting on the desktop, click or tap the Start button (or press the ⊞ key).

2. Choose Settings on the Start menu, as shown in **Figure 3-1** (your Start menu may look different).

   Turn to Chapter 1 if you need help opening an app on the Start menu.

3. The Settings screen appears, as shown in **Figure 3-2.** The Settings screen is the starting point for changing the settings here, there, and everywhere on your computer.

Choose Settings

FIGURE 3-1

4. One at a time, select each icon in the Settings screen, starting with System, to see the options available. Select the Back button (the square with the left-pointing arrow, located in the upper-left corner of the screen) to return to the Settings screen.

5. On the Settings screen, enter the word **printer** in the Find a Setting box (located at the top of the screen; refer to **Figure 3-2**). As soon as you enter the word, the Settings screen shows you a list of settings that pertain to printers. You can select a setting on the list to open the dialog box where the setting is located.

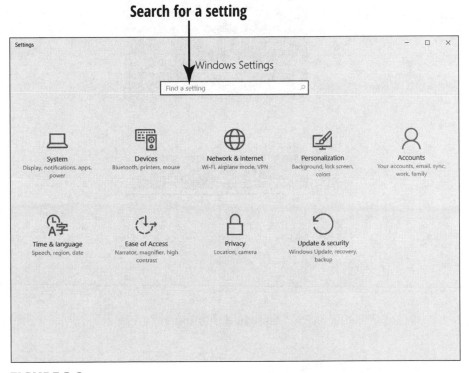

FIGURE 3-2

TIP

Windows 10 offers many different settings. Locating them can be a chore. Often the easiest way to find a setting is to enter its name in the Find a Setting box on the Settings screen.

Personalize the Lock Screen

1. On the Settings screen, select Personalization.

2. On the Personalization screen, select Lock Screen. The Lock Screen Preview screen opens. On the Background menu, choose Picture (if it isn't already chosen), as shown in **Figure 3-3.**

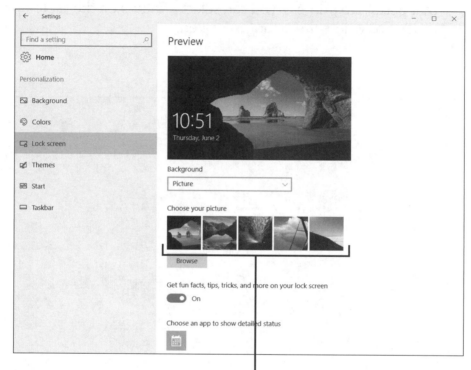

Choose a thumbnail

FIGURE 3-3

TIP

The Lock screen is the first screen you see when you start Windows 10.

3. Just above the Browse button, select each thumbnail photo, one at a time. The larger preview photo changes to show the thumbnail you selected. Select a photo that's different from the one you started with. (You can always change it later.)

TIP

You can use the Browse button to select one of your own photos from the Pictures folder. See Chapter 10 for information on adding photos to this folder and its subfolders.

Rather than see one image on the start screen, you can see a slide show of images in your Pictures folder. On the Background menu, choose Slideshow.

4. Return to the Start screen. Select your account picture (the topmost of the four icons on the left side of the Start screen) to display the menu shown in **Figure 3-4.** Then select Lock to display the Lock screen.

FIGURE 3-4

You can lock your computer anytime by pressing ⊞+L.

5. The photo you selected in Step 3 appears on the Lock screen. Display the Password screen as follows:

- **Mouse:** Click anywhere.
- **Touchscreen:** Swipe up.
- **Keyboard:** Press any key on the keyboard.

6. Enter your password, if you have one. The Windows desktop screen appears.

Choose an Account Picture

1. On the Settings screen, select Accounts. See "Access the Settings Screen," earlier in this chapter, if you need help opening the Settings screen. Your current Account picture appears in the Accounts screen,

as shown in **Figure 3-5.** (If you haven't selected a picture yet, your picture may just be an outline.)

Current account picture

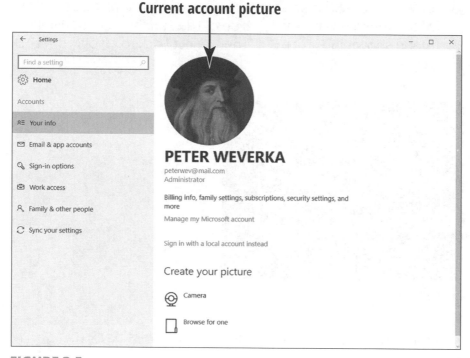

FIGURE 3-5

TIP

Your account picture appears on the password screen and the Start screen.

2. To choose one of your photos, select the Browse for One button. The contents of your Pictures folder appears in the Open dialog box. From here, you can select the Up button to access any folder on your computer or select a subfolder to open. When you find the picture you want, select it and then select the Choose Picture button. Or select Cancel to return to the previous screen without changing your account picture.

TIP

See Chapter 10 for information about adding photos to your Pictures folder.

3. If you have a built-in or attached camera (called a *webcam*), select the Camera app under Create Your Picture. The Camera app opens with

a preview of what your camera sees. See Chapter 10 for information on taking pictures with a webcam.

TIP

You may be able to use another app to select or create a picture. Select the app under Create Your Picture.

4. Return to the Start screen to see your new account picture. To return to the Start screen, click or tap the Start button or press ⊞ on your keyboard.

TIP

The easiest way to access the Accounts screen and change your account picture is through your account name. On the Start screen, select your name and then select Change Account Settings, as shown in **Figure 3-6.** Voilà! The Accounts screen appears, with Your Info selected.

Click to change your account picture

FIGURE 3-6

Check for Important Updates

1. To check for updates to Windows 10, select Update & Security on the Settings screen. See "Access the Settings screen," earlier in this chapter, if you need help getting to the PC Settings screen.

2. On the Update & Security screen, select Windows Update. The Windows Update screen appears, as shown in **Figure 3-7.**

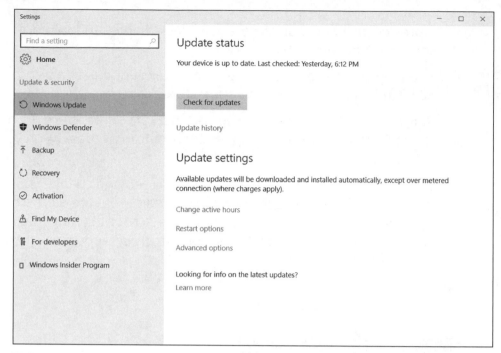

FIGURE 3-7

TIP

If you don't mind typing, you can get to the Windows Update screen by typing **windows update** in the Search box located on the taskbar.

3. The Windows Update screen informs you when Windows 10 last checked for updates and whether any were found. Select the Check for Updates button to find out whether any updates are available and update Windows 10 on your computer.

4. You may see a message that one or more updates will be downloaded and installed automatically. You do not have to do anything to install these updates — the update process is automatic. Return to the desktop to let Windows 10 manage updates automatically.

TIP

You can select the Advanced Options button on the Windows Update screen to choose how Windows 10 installs updates and get a history of updates that Windows 10 has made to your computer.

TIP

Installing an update seldom takes more than a few minutes. You can use your system during the update process. If the update process requires that you restart your computer, you see a message on the Windows Update screen and the Lock screen. If you don't restart when required, Windows 10 will automatically restart within two days of the first notification.

For information on other updates and maintaining Windows 10, see Chapter 12.

TIP

Make Windows 10 Easier to Use

1. On the Settings screen, select Ease of Access, as shown in **Figure 3-8.** (See "Access the Settings Screen" for help.) The Ease of Access screens offer many ways to make your computer, mouse, and monitor easier to use.

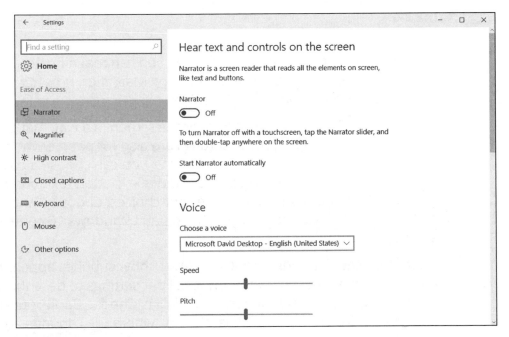

FIGURE 3-8

2. Choose Narrator settings (refer to **Figure 3-8**) to have content on the screen read aloud. These settings are for people who have difficulty reading. After turning on the Narrator switch, you choose voice, speed, and pitch settings to determine what the narrator's voice sounds like.

3. Choose Magnifier settings to enlarge what is on your computer screen. These settings are for people who have difficulty seeing. When Magnifier is turned on, the Magnifier toolbar appears onscreen. (Click or tap the magnifying glass icon to see this toolbar, if necessary.) Click or tap the plus sign on the Magnifier toolbar to zoom a portion of the screen for easier viewing, as shown in **Figure 3-9.** Click or tap the minus sign to see the screen at normal size.

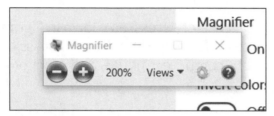

FIGURE 3-9

TIP

Without turning the Magnifier switch on, you can magnify the screen. Press ⊞ +plus key to zoom in using Magnifier. Press ⊞ +minus key to zoom out using Magnifier.

4. Choose High Contrast settings to alter the screen in a way that might make seeing text easier. These settings are also for people who have difficulty seeing. After you choose a theme, you can choose a color for text, hyperlinks, disabled text, selected text, button text, and backgrounds. Click Apply after you make your choices. Choose None and click Apply if you want to return to the default Windows 10 contrast settings.

5. Choose Closed Captions settings to control how subtitles appear in audio and video presentations. Choose Font settings to describe what you want the text in the captions to look like. Choose Background and Window settings to describe what the box where the captions appear looks like. The Preview box shows what your choices mean in real terms.

6. Choose Keyboard settings to type without using a physical keyboard. This onscreen keyboard uses the layout of a conventional keyboard. However, most people find that the standard Windows 10 virtual

keyboard is more flexible. See Chapter 1 for information on the virtual keyboard layouts.

7. Choose Mouse settings to change the size and color of the mouse pointer. As shown in **Figure 3-10,** Windows 10 offers mouse pointers of different sizes and colors. Choose the combination that tickles your fancy.

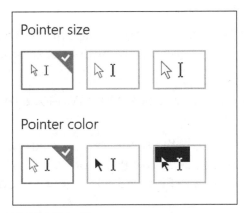

FIGURE 3-10

8. The Other Options settings control various and sundry items:

- **Play Animations in Windows** controls whether Windows apps start and close with an animation sequence. If you prefer not to see animation sequences when an app is launched or closed, turn this switch to the off position.

- **Show Windows Background** controls whether images can appear on the Start screen. If this switch is off, images don't appear on the screen, and you can't choose an image in the Personalize panel. (See the next section in this chapter, "Customize the Start Menu," for more information.)

- **Show Notifications For** controls how long certain pop-up messages appear before disappearing. These notifications are sometimes called *tooltips* or *toasts* (because of the way they pop up). By default, notifications disappear after five seconds, which usually isn't enough time to read a long notification. Note that notifications disappear when you move the mouse or select another option. I suggest that you try 30 seconds for the delay.

- **Cursor Thickness** controls the width of the vertical blinking line that appears when you can type text. The box on the left under this heading displays the current cursor (without blinking). To try a different thickness, drag the selection box to the right. (You might try a cursor thickness of 2 or 3 pixels.)

- The **Visual Notifications for Sound** options make parts of the screen "flash" when they are activated. These options are meant for the hard of hearing.

- The **Touch Feedback** options help you see when Windows recognizes that you touched the screen.

TIP

More Ease of Access settings are available through the desktop. The settings are easiest to access by pressing ⊞ U (for *usability*). In the Ease of Access Center, as shown in **Figure 3-11,** you can choose many access settings.

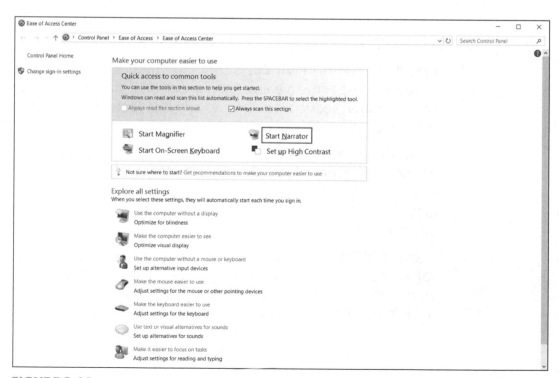

FIGURE 3-11

Customize the Start Menu

1. On the Settings screen, select Personalization. See "Access the Settings Screen," earlier in this chapter, if you need help opening the Settings screen.

2. On the Personalization screen, select Start. The Start screen opens, as shown in **Figure 3-12.** This screen offers ways to customize the Start menu and the Start screen.

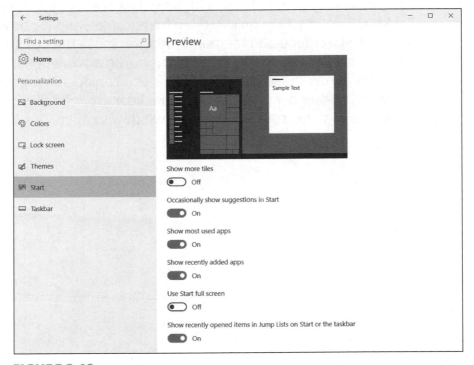

FIGURE 3-12

3. Under Start, drag the sliders to On or Off to choose what you want Windows 10 to display on the Start screen and Start menu:

   - **Show More Tiles:** Enlarges the Windows 10 Start screen. Choose this option if your Start screen is crowded with app tiles.

   - **Occasionally Show Suggestions in Start:** Places the names of apps and files on the Start screen that Windows 10 believes you want to see there.

- **Show Most Used Apps:** Places the names of programs you use most often on the Start menu. The names of these programs appear under the "Most Used" heading.

- **Show Recently Added Apps:** Places the names of apps you recently acquired on the Start menu. The names of these apps appear under the "Recently Added" heading.

- **Use Start Full Screen:** Makes the Start screen cover the entire desktop, rather than a portion of the desktop.

- **Show Recently Opened Items in Jump Lists on Start or the Taskbar:** Allows you to quickly open folders, files, and windows from the Start menu and taskbar. When you move the pointer over an app or program on the Start menu, an arrow appears; select the arrow to see a menu of items you can open. When you move the pointer over an icon on the taskbar, thumbnail windows appear so that you can choose which window to open.

Chapter 4

Working with User Accounts

Windows 10 seeks out an Internet connection automatically from the moment you start it. More often than not, you connect to the Internet using a wireless or *Wi-Fi* connection. For this reason, if you start a laptop or tablet in a coffee shop or library, you may see a notification that one or more network connections are available. That's convenient.

A computer without an Internet connection is an island, if not a paperweight. Connecting to a network, however, opens a door to your computer — and malefactors try to push through that door to access your computer. Windows 10 has a *firewall* that monitors and restricts traffic in and out. Don't be afraid of connecting to the Internet, but be aware of the risks and be careful to connect to a network that seems trustworthy. In Chapter 1, you create a local user account. You need a Microsoft Account to take full advantage of Windows 10 features such as the Microsoft Store for apps (see Chapter 9), OneDrive for online storage (see Chapter 15), and synchronized settings between computers. In this chapter, you create a Microsoft Account and choose a secure method for logging in to your account. You also discover how to switch to Airplane mode and switch from a local account to a Microsoft Account. To control access to your computer, you find out how to use a password, a shorter personal identification number (*PIN*), or even a personal photo to unlock your computer.

If other people use your computer, you may want to create more than one user account. When each person who uses the computer has a separate account, you can keep data, apps, and settings tidy and private.

Even if you're the only one using your computer, you may want more than one account. For example, if you create a new local user account, you can experiment with the new account — changing the look and function of Windows 10 — without affecting your first account.

Many of the steps in this chapter involve entering text, such as your name. If you don't have a physical keyboard, use the virtual keyboard, which is covered in Chapter 1.

Connect to the Internet

1. On the Windows desktop, look to the Network icon to see whether your computer is connected to the Internet. This icon is located to the left of the time and date readings in the lower-right corner of the screen, as shown in **Figure 4-1**.

Select or choose options by moving the mouse pointer and left-clicking or by tapping a touchscreen with your finger.

2. Select the Network icon. The Networks panel appears on the right side of your screen, as shown in **Figure 4-2,** and lists all available network connections. There may be no connections or dozens.

If you see *Not connected* and *No connections available,* you may be out of luck. Check your computer documentation to see whether your PC has wireless capability and whether you need to turn on a mechanical switch.

Network connection icon

FIGURE 4-1

TIP

If your computer is near a router (DSL or cable) and you don't have wireless capability, connect your PC and the router using an Ethernet cable, which is thicker than a phone line, with wider connections.

3. Select a connection. Note that not all displayed connections are accessible or desirable.

TIP

If you're not sure that you can trust a connection, you might want to forego a connection — better safe than sorry. (Unsafe wireless connections can be used to eavesdrop on your activities, though that scenario is rare.) However, if an available connection sports the name of the establishment you're in or near, such as a restaurant or a coffee shop, the connection may be safe. The same is true of connections at libraries, airports, and many other public spaces.

TIP

4. After you select a connection, the selected tile expands and displays the Connect Automatically check box, as shown in **Figure 4-3.** If you trust the connection and might want to use it again, leave the check box selected. Otherwise, deselect the check box. To continue, select the Connect button.

Available wireless connections

Connect automatically next time

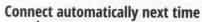

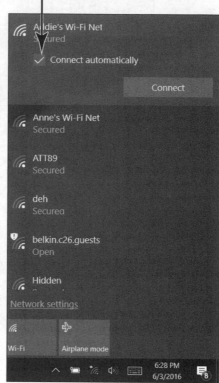

FIGURE 4-2

FIGURE 4-3

5. You may be prompted to enter a network security key (a series of characters), which limits access to those who know the key. See **Figure 4-4**. The key protects that network and its users. If you're using a hotel's connection, you can obtain the key from the front desk. If you don't know the key, select Cancel. Otherwise, enter the key (dots appear as you type) and select Next.

TIP

If the connection is public and open, you won't be prompted for a key. Open connections are common in libraries, coffee shops, and other places many people come and go.

TIP

If you have access to your *router*, which is a kind of network device connected to the phone line or cable TV, the router may have a button you can push to connect without using the security key.

A secure network requires a key

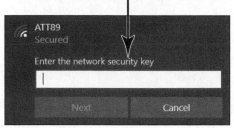

FIGURE 4-4

6. If you entered the correct key or none was required, you may see this message: *Do you want to turn on sharing between PCs and connect to devices on this network?* The term *sharing* refers to allowing computers access to your files or to a device, such as a printer. You should share at home but not in a public location. Choose one of the following:

- **No:** This option prevents you from connecting directly with other computers and protects your computer from networks in public places. You'll still have Internet access.

- **Yes:** This option enables you to share documents and devices between your computers on a home or office network.

TIP

If you're not sure about which option to choose, go with No.

7. When a Wi-Fi connection is established, *Connected* appears next to the network name in the Networks panel, as shown in **Figure 4-5**. The connection name and signal strength appear as well. The connection strength (but not the name) appears next to the time and date in the notification area in the lower-right corner of the screen (see **Figure 4-5).**

TIP

If you selected the Connect Automatically check box (in Step 4), the connection will be used anytime it is available. If you move your computer to another location out of range of this network (usually a few hundred yards), you will have to repeat these steps to connect to another network.

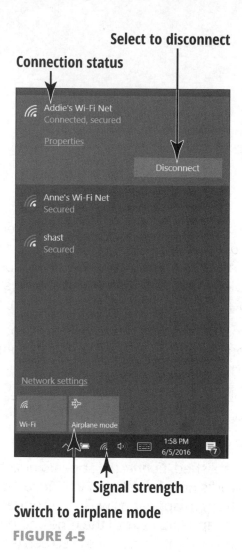

Connection status

Select to disconnect

Signal strength

Switch to airplane mode

FIGURE 4-5

Disconnect or Switch to Airplane Mode

1. Most of the time, you'll stay connected to the network. When you shut down the computer or move the computer far enough away from the connection, it disconnects automatically. To turn off or disconnect the network connection, display the Networks panel again (refer to **Figure 4-5**).

2. Select the connected network (refer to **Figure 4-5**) and then select the Disconnect button. (If you disconnect this network, reconnect before continuing.)

3. For safety's sake, the airlines don't want passengers to send or receive wireless data signals while the airplane is in flight; these signals can interfere with the airplane's communications systems. This is why the captain gives the order to "turn off all electrical devices." Rather than turn off your computer, however, you can switch to Airplane mode. To do so, open the Networks panel and select the Airplane Mode button (see **Figure 4-5**).

4. In Airplane mode, an airplane icon appears to the left of the time and date readings in the lower-right corner of the screen, as shown in **Figure 4-6**. In Airplane mode, your computer doesn't send wireless data signals. To switch out of Airplane mode and reconnect to the Internet, select the airplane icon to display the Network panel. Then select the Airplane Mode button (refer to **Figure 4-6**).

Select to turn off Airplane mode

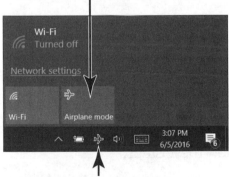

Airplane mode icon

FIGURE 4-6

TIP

Switching to Airplane mode is much more convenient than turning off your computer's network connection and turning it back on again. It takes but a second or two.

Create a New Microsoft Account

Follow these steps to switch your Windows 10 user account from a local account to a Microsoft Account and in so doing create a Microsoft account:

1. On the Start screen, select your picture on the left side of the screen. In the pop-up menu that appears (see **Figure 4-7**), choose Change Account Settings. The Settings app opens to the Accounts screen. Your account information appears with *Local Account* under your name, as shown in **Figure 4-8**.

Select for fast access to the Accounts screen

FIGURE 4-7

TIP

If you see don't see *Local Account*, you already have a Microsoft Account and don't need to follow these steps.

2. Select the Sign In with a Microsoft Account Instead link. If you have a password, enter it and select Next. The Make It Yours screen appears. To create a new account, select the Create One! link.

3. On the Let's Create Your Account screen (see **Figure 4-9**), type your first and last names in the appropriate boxes.

4. In the Email Address box, type the email address you want to use for this account. Microsoft will send notices about the Microsoft Account to the address you enter.

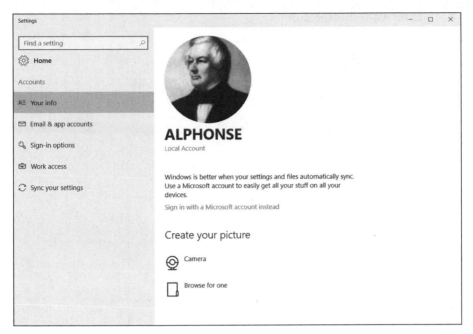

FIGURE 4-8

TIP

5. In the Password box, type a password. Dots appear instead of what you type. Use at least eight characters including at least two upper-case letters, two lowercase letters, two numbers, or two symbols. No spaces are allowed.

Your password should be easy enough for you to remember and type, but not easy for someone else to guess. Don't use the names of any family members (including pets). A good password can be difficult to create, so try this trick: Think of a memorable phrase or lyric. Next, use the first letter from each word, capitalizing some of those letters. Then substitute some letters with numbers (for example, 3 for the letter *E* or the number 0 for the letter *O*). Don't put your password on a sticky note near your screen.

6. If your country or region is not preselected, select your country.

Select the month, day, and year of your birth. (You can lie, but be sure to remember your response.)

Enter your information

FIGURE 4-9

7. Review your entries. Select the Next button.

8. On the See What's Most Relevant to You screen, shown in **Figure 4-10**, select the first check box if you want to allow Microsoft to monitor your online activity so that it can target online advertisements to your screen based on your user profile and history of surfing the web.

9. If you don't want to receive promotional offers and surveys, select the check box to remove the check mark from the second check box.

TIP

10. Select the Next button. The Enter Your Old Password screen appears. Enter the password to your local account, if you had a password. Then click Next. Congratulations! You just created a Microsoft Account.

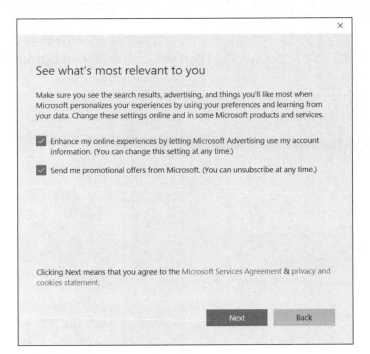

FIGURE 4-10

Switch from a Local to an Existing Microsoft Account

1. Follow these steps to switch your Windows 10 user account from a local account to your existing Microsoft Account. On the Start screen, select your name in the upper-left corner of the screen and then choose Change Account Settings from the pop-up menu that appears (refer to **Figure 4-7**). The Accounts screen opens. Your account information appears with *Local Account* under your name (refer to **Figure 4-8**).

TIP If you don't have a Microsoft Account already, see "Create a New Microsoft Account," earlier in this chapter.

TIP If you don't see *Local Account* under your user account name, you're already signed in with your Microsoft Account.

2. Select the Sign In with a Microsoft Account Instead link. The screen shown in **Figure 4-11** appears. Type the email address of your

Microsoft Account (or the phone number associated with the account) as well as the password. Then select the Sign In button.

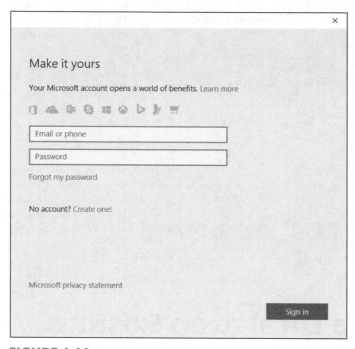

FIGURE 4-11

3. Confirm the Security verification data. When you set up your Microsoft Account, you chose how to receive the code you need to activate your Microsoft Account by email or by phone. Select Next.

4. The Enter the Code You Received screen appears. Open your email service and obtain the code. It arrives in an email from the Microsoft Account Team. Enter the code and choose Next until you come to the Switch to a Microsoft Account on This PC screen. Select the Switch button. Note your account name and associated email address on the Accounts screen.

Add a User Account

1. You already have the only user account you require on your computer. However, you may want to create an account for someone in your household or as a practice account. Select your name on the Start screen. Choose Change Account Settings from the menu that appears (refer to **Figure 4-7**). The Settings app opens to the Accounts screen.

2. On the left, select Family & Other People. On the right, select Add Someone Else to This PC. The How Will This Person Sign In screen appears.

If you can't select Add an Account, return to the Start screen. Select your name and choose Sign Out. On the Sign In screen, choose the account you created in Chapter 1.

3. At the bottom of the How Will This Person Sign In screen, select the link called I Don't Have This Person's Sign-In Information.

If you know you want a Microsoft Account instead of a local account, jump to "Create a New Microsoft Account" or "Switch from a Local to an Existing Microsoft Account," earlier in this chapter.

4. On the next screen, (it's called Let's Create Your Account), go to the bottom of the screen and click or tap the Add a User without a Microsoft Account link.

5. On the next screen, enter the user name in the first box, as shown in **Figure 4-12**. Use the person's first name, last name, first and last name, initials, nickname — something easy to remember and type.

You are not required to use a password with a local account, which makes signing in easy. However, without a password, anyone can use the computer and access information you might want to protect.

6. In the Password box, enter a password. Dots will appear for each character you type.

For suggestions on creating a good password, see the tip in Step 5 in the section, "Create a New Microsoft Account," earlier in this chapter.

7. In the Reenter Password box, type the same password exactly.

8. In the Password Hint box, type a reminder that only you will understand.

For laptops or other portable devices, consider using your phone number with area code as the hint (if you're sure you don't need a real hint). The hint appears when someone tries and fails to enter login information. By including your phone number, you might help an honest person return your lost, stolen, or misplaced device to you.

Only the user name is required for a local account

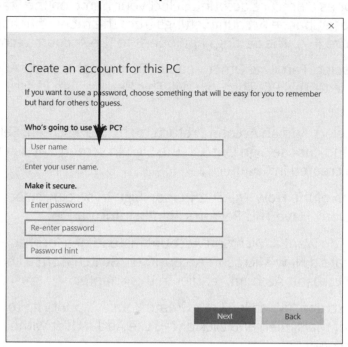

FIGURE 4-12

9. After completing all the available boxes, choose the Next button. You may see an error message if you left a required field empty, your passwords don't match, or the user name already exists on this computer. If you do see an error, correct your mistake and choose Next again.

10. In the Accounts screen, the new user name appears under Other People, as shown in **Figure 4-13**.

11. Return to the Start screen. In the upper-left corner of the screen, select your user name. Notice that the new user name appears on the drop-down menu. You can switch between accounts by selecting a user name on the drop-down menu. To sign out of an account, choose Sign Out.

12. In the drop-down menu, select the new user name to switch to that account.

13. A screen appears with the new user name. If you used a password on the new user account, type that password in the box and select the onscreen right arrow or press Enter.

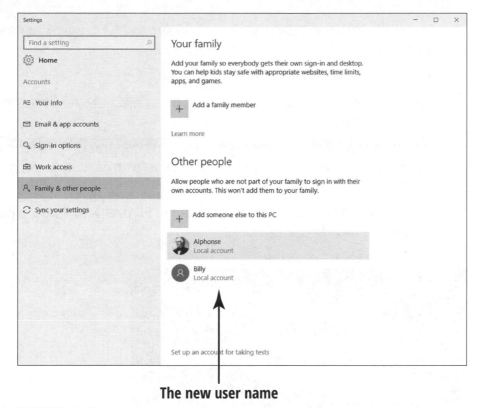

The new user name

FIGURE 4-13

The first time you sign in as a new user, you have to wait a moment while apps are installed for the new user. Soon the generic Start screen appears. (Any settings you changed in your account do not transfer to other accounts.)

TIP

For information on personalizing the Lock and Start screens for the new account, see Chapter 3.

TIP

Create a Password

1. On the Start screen, select your name. From the drop-down menu that appears, choose Change Account Settings (refer to **Figure 4-6**). The Settings app opens to the Accounts screen.

TIP

If you already have a password, see the section "Change or Remove Your Password."

2. On the left, select Sign-in Options.

3. If you don't have a password but want one, select the Add button under Password.

TIP

The buttons available under Sign-in Options depend on your current setup. You may see buttons that enable you to create, change, or remove a particular setting.

4. In the Create a Password screen, shown in **Figure 4-14**, enter a password in the New Password box.

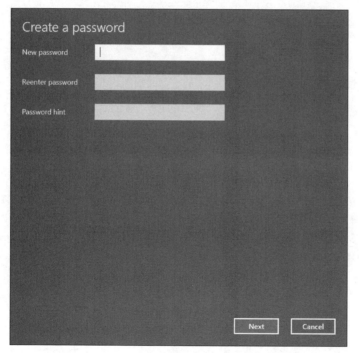

Create a password

New password

Reenter password

Password hint

Next   Cancel

FIGURE 4-14

TIP

For a local account, the password can be any length. See Step 5 in the "Create a New Microsoft Account" section for suggestions about creating a good password.

5. In the Reenter Password box, enter the password again.

6. Enter a hint to remind yourself — and no one else — about your password.

7. Select Next. If any error messages appear, correct the entries and select Next again.

8. The final Create a Password screen indicates that you must use your new password the next time you sign in. Select Finish.

Change or Remove Your Password

1. On the Start screen, select your name, and then choose Change Account Settings. On the left side of the Accounts screen, select Sign-in Options.

2. If you want to change your password, select the Change button.

If you don't have a password but want one, see the preceding "Create a Password" section.

TIP

3. On the Change Your Password screen, enter your current password and then select the Next button.

4. On the next Change Your Password screen (see **Figure 4-15**), enter the new password.

To remove your current password and use no password, leave all boxes blank. However, especially if you have a laptop that you carry with you, going without a password isn't recommended. Without a password to safeguard it, anyone can get into your laptop.

TIP

For a local account, the password can be any length. Microsoft Account passwords must be between 7 and 16 characters and sufficiently complex, as determined by Windows 10.

5. In the Reenter Password box, enter the password again.

6. Enter a hint to remind yourself — and no one else — about your password. Then select Next. If any error messages appear, correct the entries and select Next again.

7. The final screen indicates you must use your new password the next time you sign in. (This message appears even if you left the password blank, in which case you won't need any password.) Select Finish.

If you don't want a password, leave these boxes blank

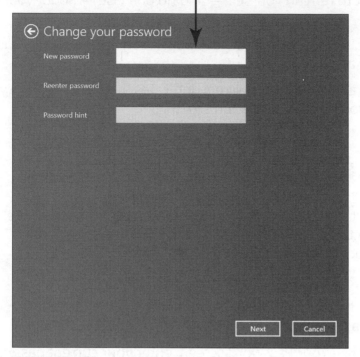

FIGURE 4-15

Create a PIN

1. A *PIN* (personal identification number) has two advantages over a password. One, a PIN consists of numbers, so it's easier to remember and enter, especially with a virtual keyboard. Two, you don't press the Enter key with a PIN, making it even faster to use. (I use a PIN on my home computer.) On the Start screen, select your user name and then choose Change Account Settings.

2. On the Accounts screen, select Sign-in Options. Select the Add button under PIN.

If you have a PIN but want to change or remove it, see the section "Change Your Pin."

TIP

You can't create a picture password or PIN if you don't have a regular password. See the section "Create a Password."

3. On the next screen, enter your current password and then select OK.

TIP

4. On the Set Up a PIN screen, shown in **Figure 4-16**, enter digits in the first box. Reenter those digits in the second box. Select OK. The next time you sign in, enter your PIN.

FIGURE 4-16

TIP

On the sign-in screen, you can switch to a password screen, even if you have a PIN. This feature enables you to sign in in case you don't remember your PIN.

Change Your PIN

1. Select your name on the Start screen and then choose Change Account Settings. On the Accounts screen, select Sign-in Options.

TIP

If you don't have a PIN but want one, see the preceding section, "Create a PIN."

2. Select the Change button.

3. Enter your current PIN in the Change Your Pin screen.

4. Enter a new four-digit PIN in the first box.

5. In the Confirm PIN box, reenter your new PIN. (A message appears if the PINs don't match.)

6. Select Finish. The next time you sign in, enter your new PIN.

Delete a User Account

1. Before you delete a user account, make sure that the user of that account is signed out. Then sign in to the administrator account, which is the one you create in Chapter 1.

2. Select your name on the Start screen and then choose Change Account Settings. On the Accounts screen, select Family & Other People (see **Figure 4-17**).

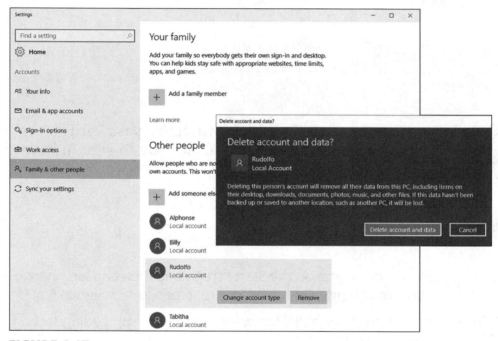

FIGURE 4-17

3. Select the account you want to delete. Then select the Remove button.

4. In the Delete Account and Data window, select the Delete Account and Data button.

TIP

Take heed of the onscreen warning. Deleting a user account removes the user's data, including all documents, music, and other files. If you're not sure which option is best, choose Cancel.

Chapter 5

Getting Comfortable with the Desktop

The *desktop* is Grand Central Station as far as Windows 10 is concerned. Sure, you can open applications from the Start screen (Chapter 2 explains how), but with a few simple modifications, you can open applications from the desktop as well. When you're running more than one application, you can go to the desktop and quickly switch from one application to another. In fact, in Windows 10, you can create a second "virtual" desktop for one set of open applications (applications that pertain to leisure, let's say), and when the boss isn't looking, you can switch to the second desktop to play games or chat with friends.

One key feature of the desktop is the *taskbar,* a strip along the bottom of the screen that shows icons for desktop programs. The taskbar can be used to run and switch between desktop programs. Most programs on the desktop run in windows, as opposed to the full-screen nature of Windows 10 apps.

In this chapter, you get acquainted with the desktop, the taskbar, and windowed apps. You change the date, time, and time zone, as needed. You resize and reposition windowed apps, and discover how to "add a desktop" for a second set of open applications. You select a background for the desktop and make some desktop apps more convenient to use by pinning them to the taskbar. Finally, you work with the Task Manager, which lets you end any app — desktop or Windows 10.

The desktop originated when using the mouse was the most common method for selecting objects (touchscreens were nonexistent). Therefore, on the desktop, a few tasks are easier to do with the mouse than with touch or keyboard.

This chapter is an introduction to the desktop. See Part 4 to dive a little deeper into desktop functions, such as organizing documents.

Check Out the Desktop

1. Go to the desktop (if you aren't already there) by using one of these techniques:

   - On the Start screen, select the Desktop tile.

   - With the Start screen open, display the desktop simply by clicking or tapping the Windows button (it's located in the lower-left corner of your computer screen).

   - Press ⊞+D.

   - Right-click the Windows button and choose Desktop on the pop-up menu that appears.

2. Your desktop has a picture in the background. Examine your desktop for *icons* — small pictures that represent either programs, which perform functions, or documents, such as letters and photos. You select an icon to run a program or open a document. The Windows 10 desktop displays an icon for the Recycle Bin, where deleted documents go. The Recycle Bin may be the only icon on your desktop, or you may see others. See Chapter 14 for information on using the Recycle Bin.

3. The area at the bottom of the screen is the *taskbar,* shown in **Figure 5-1**. From left to right, the taskbar offers these amenities:

- **Windows button:** Selecting this button opens the Start screen. (Click or Tap the button a second time to close the Start screen.)

- **Search the Web and Windows box:** You can enter a search term here to look for Windows settings, applications, files on your computer, and information on the Internet. See Chapter 2 for information about using this part of the taskbar to ask questions of Cortana, the talking digital assistant.

- **Task View icon:** Selecting this icon brings up thumbnail images of applications currently running on your computer. You can select an application thumbnail to switch to an application. You can also select New Desktop to open a second desktop (see "Open a Second Desktop," later in this chapter, for more information).

- **Icons:** Some icons appear on the taskbar automatically. Very likely, your taskbar has icons for File Explorer and Edge. You can select these icons to open File Explorer and Edge. When you open an application, Windows 10 places its icon on the taskbar.

- **Icon tray:** The *icon tray* displays icons for programs that run automatically when your computer starts. The date and time are to the right of the icon tray.

You can use the taskbar to switch between programs by selecting the icon for the program you want to use.

TIP

4. Select an icon in the icon tray to open the associated program. (Refer to **Figure 5-1** if you aren't sure where the icon tray is located.)

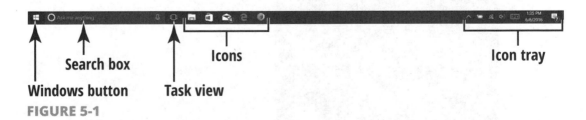

Search box

Windows button   **Task view**   **Icons**   **Icon tray**

FIGURE 5-1

You select items on the desktop or in the taskbar by clicking with the mouse or tapping the touchscreen. To some extent, you can use the Tab and arrow keys, but that's an awkward method.

If you have a touchscreen, note the taskbar icon for the virtual keyboard. See Chapter 1 for information about using the keyboard.

5. Right-click over an icon or tap and hold until a small box appears, and then release. A *context menu* appears with options specific to the icon you selected. Select anywhere else on the desktop to dismiss this menu. Repeat this on a few different areas of the screen to see how the context menu changes.

Change the Date or Time

1. Select the date and time displayed in the taskbar. A calendar and clock pop up, as shown in **Figure 5-2**.

FIGURE 5-2

2. If the date or time is incorrect for your location, select the Windows button and then select the Settings button on the left side of the Start screen. The Settings screen opens. Select Time & Language. You see the Date and Time window, shown in **Figure 5-3, left.**

Select your time zone

Turn off automatic time   **Set the time**

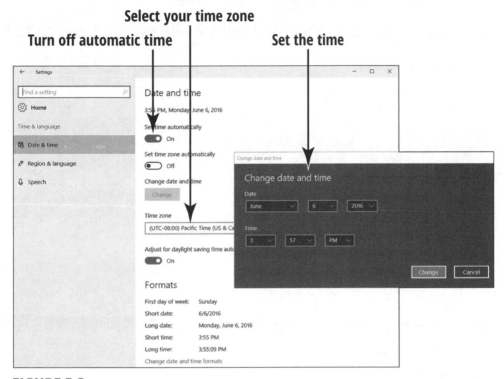

FIGURE 5-3

3. Windows 10 determines the correct time and date from the Internet, and your computer should show the right time and date, but if it doesn't, turn off the Set Time Automatically option and select the Change button. You see the Change Date and Time screen (see **Figure 5-3**). Select the correct date and time in this screen. Change the time by using the little triangles that point up (later) or down (earlier) or by entering the specific hours and minutes. Select Change to keep your change or Cancel to ignore your change.

4. Back in the Date and Time window, select your Time Zone from the drop-down list, if necessary. Turn the Adjust for Daylight Saving Time option on or off as appropriate.

5. To change the format with which the time and date are displayed in the lower-right corner of the screen, select the Change Date and Time Formats link in the Date and Time window. Then, in the Change Date and Time Formats window (see **Figure 5-4**), choose how you want the date and time to be displayed on your computer screen.

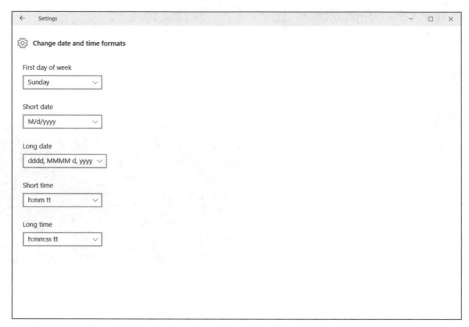

FIGURE 5-4

Explore the Parts of a Window

1. In the taskbar, select the File Explorer icon (it looks like a folder). File Explorer opens, as shown in **Figure 5-5**.

TIP

File Explorer enables you to view your computer storage, such as hard disks, and folders, which are used to organize your documents. See Chapter 14 for information on using File Explorer.

2. Explore the example window in **Figure 5-5,** starting at the top left:

   • **Quick Access toolbar:** The *Quick Access toolbar* gives you fast access to common operations, such as creating a new folder. This toolbar is not present in all windows and may feature different functions, depending on the window.

- **Title bar:** The *title bar,* which is the top line of the window, lists the name of the file or folder that is currently open.

TIP

The title of the window in **Figure 5-5** is This PC, the location File **Explorer is focused on when you open File Explorer.**

Quick Access toolbar   File Explorer window

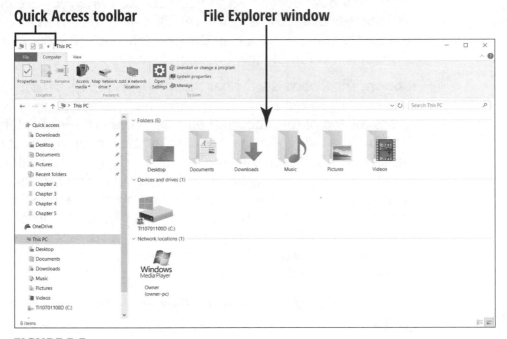

FIGURE 5-5

- **Minimize:** The *Minimize button* shrinks or hides the window's contents. The program that the window contains is still running and open, but the window is out of sight. You'll still see the program's icon in the taskbar. Select the Minimize button when you want to ignore a particular window but aren't actually done with it. To restore the window, select its icon in the taskbar.

- **Maximize/Restore:** The *Maximize button* (the button with a single square) fills the screen with the contents of the window. Select the Maximize button to hide the desktop and other open windows, to concentrate on one window, and to see as much of the window's contents as you can. The *Restore button* (the button with two squares) is the name of the button that appears after you select the Maximize button; it replaces the Maximize button. Select the Restore button to return the window to its previous size, which is between maximized and minimized. (Press +up-arrow key to maximize, and + down-arrow key to restore or minimize.)

- **Close:** The *Close button* is the button with the X in the top-right corner of the window. Select the Close button when you are done with the window. Close is also called Quit and Exit. (Press Alt+F4 to close the current window or the desktop itself. This keyboard shortcut works for Windows 10 apps, as well.)

- **Ribbon:** The *Ribbon* is a toolbar that provides access to many functions organized as groups within tabs. The tabs appear across the top of the Ribbon. The first time you run File Explorer, the Ribbon is hidden (collapsed). Display the Ribbon by selecting the caret symbol (^) on the far right, next to Help (the question mark). Select the caret again to hide the Ribbon. You can also press Ctrl+F1 to toggle the Ribbon on and off. (Leave the Ribbon visible for this chapter.) The tabs remain in view and function the same. Although Ribbons vary between programs, most Ribbons have File and View tabs. To use a tab, select its name to display its functions, and then select the item you want to use.

TIP

The Ribbon can help you discover new functions.

- **Contents:** The bulk of the window contains the program or document you're using. File Explorer displays locations on the left and objects in that location on the right.

- **Status bar:** Along the bottom edge of the window, some programs display information about the window or its contents in a single-line *status bar.* File Explorer lists how many files are in the currently open folder and how many files (if any) have been selected.

TIP

Scan the edges of windows. Often, important information and functions are pushed to these edges around the main content area.

3. Select the Close button (the X) to close File Explorer.

Although the Quick Access toolbar and the Close button work on a touchscreen, they are small targets. You may find a stylus more accurate when dealing with smaller elements.

See Chapter 2 for information on finding other desktop programs, such as the Calculator.

Resize a Window

1. To resize a window, open File Explorer by selecting the folder icon in the taskbar. (Refer to **Figure 5-5**.)

2. If the window is maximized (fills the screen), select the Restore button to make the window smaller.

3. Use one of these methods to resize the window:

   • **Mouse:** Move the mouse pointer to the right edge of the window until the pointer changes to a double-headed arrow, called the *resize pointer*. Click and drag the edge of the window, using the resize pointer. (To drag, click and hold down the mouse button while you move the mouse.)

   • **Touchscreen:** Drag the right edge of the window.

   Drag left to shrink the window and right to expand it.

4. Resize the window's width and height at the same time by dragging a corner of the window (see **Figure 5-6**). If you want a challenge, try resizing the top-right corner without accidentally selecting the Close button.

5. Resize the window's width *or* height by dragging any of the four sides.

   You may want to resize a window to show only what you need to see, nothing more. Practice resizing from any side or corner.

6. Leave the window open as you go on to the next task.

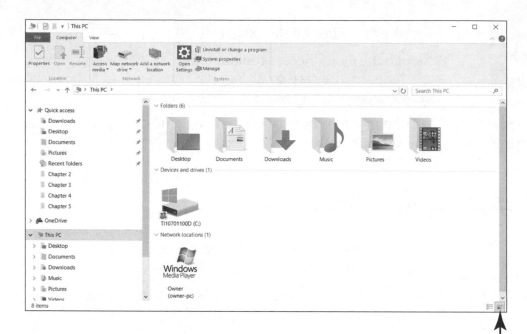

Drag the corner with your mouse or your finger to resize the window

FIGURE 5-6

Arrange Some Windows

1. On the desktop, select and open the Recycle Bin by double-clicking or double-tapping its icon. The Recycle Bin contains deleted files and folders. It appears in another File Explorer window. See **Figure 5-7**.

TIP

Double-click by clicking the left mouse button twice, without a pause. Double-tap by tapping twice in quick succession.

2. If File Explorer isn't still open from the preceding section, open it by selecting the folder icon in the taskbar. You now see two overlapping windows on the desktop (refer to **Figure 5-7**), one titled *This PC* and the other titled *Recycle Bin*.

TIP

The window in front of the others is called the *active* window. All other windows are *inactive*. Note that the title bar of the active window is a different color from the title bar in any inactive window. Selecting anywhere in an inactive window makes it active and moves it to the front of the others.

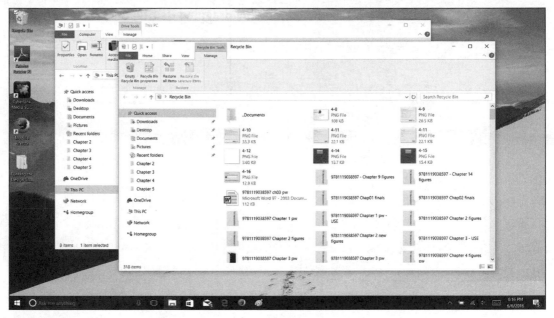

FIGURE 5-7

3. Drag the Recycle Bin title bar (avoiding the buttons on the left and right ends) to move that window a little.

4. Drag the This PC title bar (again, avoiding the buttons on both ends). The This PC window moves in front of the Recycle Bin as you move it. Move both windows so that you can see a little of each, as in **Figure 5-8**.

5. Practice moving both windows. Arranging windows helps you see and do more than one thing at a time. Use the techniques from the preceding section, "Resize a Window," to see as much as you can of both windows at one time.

If you can't see the title bar of the window you want to move, move the other window to uncover the hidden title bar.

TIP

6. Leave both windows open for the following task.

Move a window by dragging its title bar

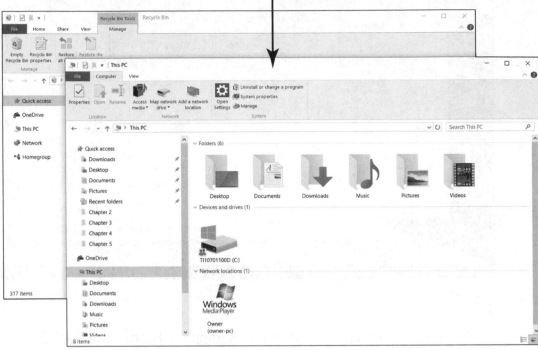

FIGURE 5-8

Snap a Window

1. Drag one of the windows you worked with in the preceding section to the left edge of the screen. When the mouse pointer or your finger reaches the left edge of the screen, you see an outline on the screen, as shown in **Figure 5-9.** When you release the mouse or your finger, the window resizes automatically to fill the left half of the screen, as shown in **Figure 5-10.** This procedure is called *snap*. (To snap a window using the keyboard, press ■+left arrow to snap a window to the left; press ■+right arrow to snap a window to the right.)

2. After you snap the first open window, the second open window appears in thumbnail form (see **Figure 5-10**). Tap or click this second window thumbnail to make it fill, or snap to, the right side of the window.

When two or more windows are displayed side by side like this, they are called *tiled* windows.

TIP

Drag the window to the far left

Note the outline

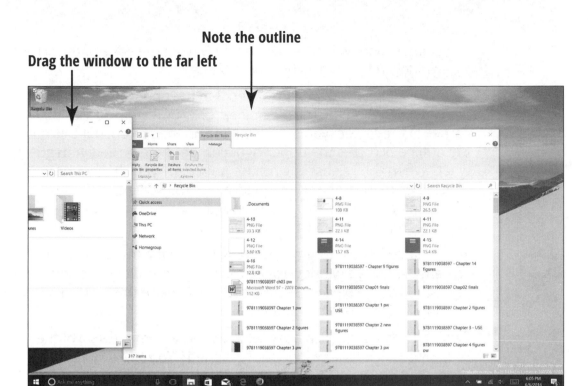

FIGURE 5-9

Tap or click to snap the other window

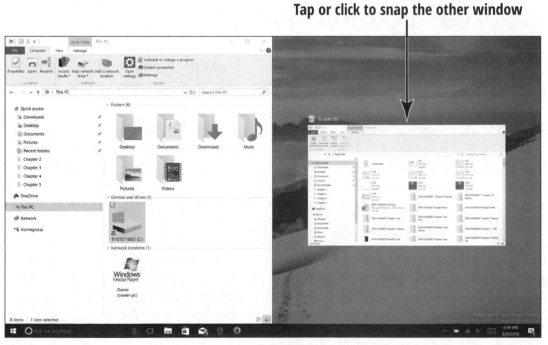

FIGURE 5-10

3. Drag either window by the title bar away from the edge of the screen. The window returns to its previous size.

4. Drag the window you moved in Step 3 to the upper-right corner of the window. When the mouse pointer or your finger touches the corner of the screen, you see an outline on the screen, but this time the outline occupies the upper-right corner of the screen. And guess what? When you release the mouse pointer or your finger, the window snaps to the upper-right quadrant of the screen. In this way, by snapping windows to the corner of the screen, you can tile four windows on your screen, not two windows.

TIP

You can maximize a window by dragging it to the top edge of the screen. Dragging a window to the top is the equivalent of selecting the Maximize button (see the section "Explore the Parts of a Window," earlier in this chapter).

5. Drag the title bar of each open window away from the side of the screen so that neither window is "snapped." You'll need these open windows if you want to move on to "Open a Second Desktop," the next topic in this chapter.

Open a Second Desktop

1. If File Explorer and Recycle Bin aren't open on your desktop (because you didn't follow the previous exercise in this chapter), open those programs now.

2. Select the Task View button on the taskbar. As Chapter 2 explains, you can use this button to switch between open application windows. After you select the Task View button, thumbnail versions of open windows appear on the desktop. At this point, you can select a thumbnail to go to a different application, but don't do that just yet.

TIP

You can press ⊞+Tab to select the Task View button.

3. Notice the New Desktop button that appears after you select the Task View button. Select the New Desktop button now. As shown in **Figure 5-11**, two desktop tiles appear at the bottom of the screen. The desktop tiles are labeled "Desktop 1" and "Desktop 2."

Go to a different desktop   **New Desktop button**

FIGURE 5-11

4. Select Desktop 2. You see a brand-new, pristine desktop. Congratulations; you are now in Desktop 2. Create a second (or third or fourth) desktop when you want to keep the first desktop from getting crowded with too many applications or to better organize your work. For example, if you are using applications for your work and using other applications for leisure purposes, put the work applications on one desktop and the leisure applications on another. This will help you find the application you want to work with.

5. While you are on Desktop 2, open the Photos app. Having just one application on the desktop makes working with that application a little easier.

6. Select the Task View button again. You can see, on the Desktop 2 tile, the Photos app.

7. Move the pointer or your finger onto the Desktop 2 tile, and when the Close button appears (refer to **Figure 5-11**), click or tap the Close

button to close Desktop 2. The Photos app that you opened on Desktop 2 now appears on Desktop 1, the only open desktop. When you close a desktop, all its open applications move to the desktop that is still open.

Choose a Desktop Background

1. Select the Windows button to open the Start menu. Then, on the Start menu, choose Settings to open the Settings window.

2. Select Personalization. Then, in the Personalization window, select Background (if it isn't already selected). The Background screen, as shown in **Figure 5-12**, is the place to go to choose a background for the Windows desktop.

You can use the Personalization window to customize many aspects of the desktop. The more time you spend on the desktop, the more worthwhile this personalization may be.

TIP

3. In the Personalization window, select Picture on the Background menu (see **Figure 5-12**).

4. Select any photo to make that photo the desktop background. The background changes immediately. To see the entire desktop, minimize the Settings window. Restore the Settings window by selecting its icon in the taskbar or by repeating the preceding steps.

To use a photo of your own as the desktop background, select the Browse button and choose a photo in the Open dialog box.

TIP

5. On the Background menu, choose Solid Color to experiment with making a solid color the desktop background. After you choose Solid Color, a color palette appears in the Personalization screen (see **Figure 5-12**). Select a color in the color palette. The background changes immediately. What do you think of having a color background? You can minimize the Settings window to get a good look at your new desktop background.

6. Choose the background you like best — a picture or a color — on the Personalization screen and then close the Settings window.

Choose a picture

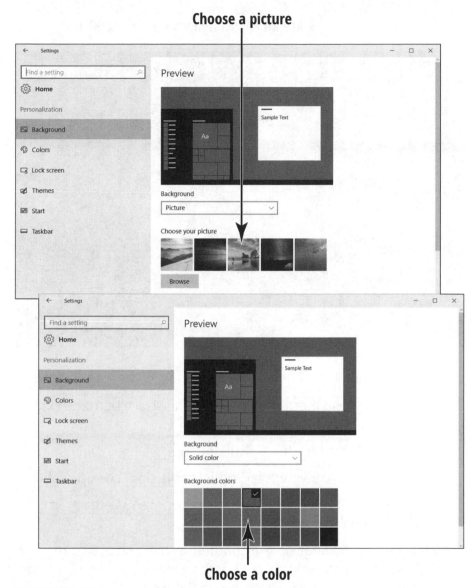

Choose a color

FIGURE 5-12

Pin Icons to the Taskbar

1. On the Start screen, scroll to the Calculator tile, as shown in **Figure 5-13**.

Place an application icon on the taskbar

FIGURE 5-13

2. Use one of these methods to display the shortcut menu on the Calculator tile:

- **Mouse:** Right-click the Calculator tile.
- **Touchscreen:** Swipe the Calculator tile down or up slightly.

3. Select More on the shortcut menu. A submenu with more options appears (see **Figure 5-13**).

4. Select Pin to Taskbar on the submenu. Doing so places the icon for Calculator in the desktop taskbar for easy access. The Calculator icon appears in the taskbar, as shown in **Figure 5-14**.

TIP

Press 🪟+D to go directly to the desktop at any time.

5. Repeat Steps 1 and 3 and then select Unpin from Taskbar.

Calculator is pinned

FIGURE 5-14

TIP

A fast way to remove an icon from the taskbar is to right-click it and choose Unpin from Taskbar on the shortcut menu.

6. Switch to the desktop. The Calculator icon is gone.

TIP

You can pin desktop apps to the Start screen in addition to or instead of the desktop. Windows 10 apps can be pinned only to the Start screen.

TIP

Pinned icons have a killer feature: *jumplists,* which are short menus of tasks and documents specific to the pinned app. To see the jumplist of a pinned app, right-click its icon in the taskbar or tap and hold on the icon until a small box appears. Try that with the File Explorer icon in the taskbar. Not all desktop apps have jumplists.

Stop Apps with the Task Manager

1. On the desktop, select Task Manager from the taskbar context menu (shown in **Figure 5-15**) using one of these methods:

   • **Mouse:** Right-click over an empty area of the taskbar and select Task Manager from the context menu.

   • **Touchscreen:** Tap and hold an empty area of the taskbar until a small box appears; then release. Select Task Manager from the context menu.

Taskbar context menu

FIGURE 5-15

- **Keyboard:** Press Ctrl+Shift+Esc to display the Task Manager directly.

2. The Task Manager lists any running apps — both desktop apps and Windows 10 apps. Select an app, also referred to as a *task*. Note that the End Task button is now available, as shown in **Figure 5-16**. You don't have to end this task, but you could. Any of the tasks in the Task Manager window can be ended without consequences.

Select a task

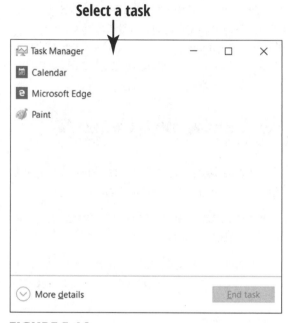

FIGURE 5-16

TIP

Be careful about ending an app used to create something (for example, a word-processing app) because you could lose data you haven't saved before ending the task. Use the Task Manager to end tasks that you can't end otherwise, such as a frozen or locked app or one that seems to slow down everything.

3. Select the More Details option. The Task Manager expands and displays detailed information about every process running on the computer. There's more to Task Manager, although you may not need all of its capabilities. Select Fewer Details to return to the simpler version.

4. Close the Task Manager.

2

Windows 10 and the Web

Explore the Internet.

Send and receive email.

Test-drive some valuable apps.

Chapter 6

Finding What You Need on the Web

The World Wide Web — or, simply, the web — provides quick access to information and entertainment worldwide. One part library, one part marketplace, and one part soapbox, the web makes everything equidistant: From down the block to halfway around the world — even out into space — everything is a few clicks or taps away. News, shopping, and the electronic equivalent of the town square await you.

You explore the web using a *web browser,* a program designed to make browsing the web easy, enjoyable, and safe. In this chapter, I show how you can use the Edge browser to step beyond your computer into the global village.

You browse *web pages*, which are published by governments, businesses, and individuals — anyone can create web pages. Each web page may consist of a few words or thousands of words and pictures. A web page is part of a larger collection called a *website,* which consists of a group of related web pages published on a topic by an organization or individual. Companies and individuals create websites to organize their related pages.

Pages and sites on the web have some common characteristics:

>> **Unique addresses,** which are formally called *URLs* (URL stands for Uniform Resource Locator, in case you're ever on *Jeopardy!*).

>> **Connecting links** that move you from page to page when you select them. These *links* (also called *hypertext links* or *hyperlinks*) often appear underlined and blue. Pictures and other graphic images can also be links to other pages. You can tell when a picture or image is a link by moving the pointer over it. The pointer changes from an arrow to a hand when it is over a hyperlink picture or image. Exploring the web using links is easier than typing URLs.

In this chapter, you use Edge to browse the web. To get the most out of browsing, you juggle multiple sites simultaneously and find out how to bookmark your favorite websites. You also find out how to search for almost anything, make use of some nice features in Edge, and use the Reader app to examine a PDF file.

TIP

Edge is by no means the only browser. Microsoft invented Edge to coincide with the release of Windows 10. You are hereby encouraged to test-drive other, more established browsers, namely Mozilla Firefox (www.mozilla.org) and Chrome (www.google.com/chrome/browser).

Browse the Web with Edge

1. Open Edge by selecting its tile on the Start screen or its icon on the taskbar. Edge opens to the *start page,* as shown in **Figure 6-1**. This page presents websites and news stories that Microsoft thinks are of interest to you based on your browsing history. If you haven't used Edge yet or haven't used it very often, you don't have a browsing history to speak of, and the websites and news stories you see here probably look quite tepid. (Later in this chapter, "Explore Edge Features" explains how to choose what web pages you see when you start Edge.)

Address bar

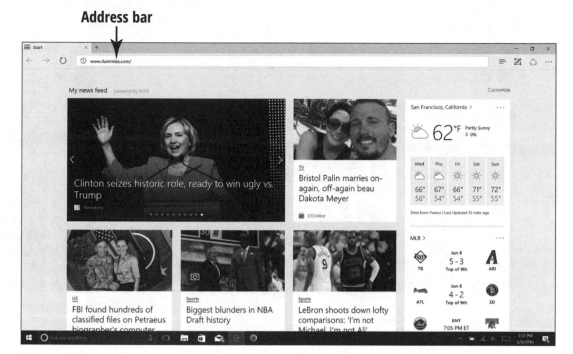

FIGURE 6-1

TIP

When you start Edge, you may see an error message if you're not connected to the Internet. If so, see Chapter 4 for information on connecting. See "Bookmark and Revisit Your Favorite Websites," later in this chapter, for instructions about choosing a home page.

2. Note the *address bar* at the top of the Edge screen (refer to **Figure 6-1**). In the address box, type `www.dummies.com`. As you type, search suggestions appear in a drop-down menu. Either select `www.dummies.com` in the search suggestions or press Enter. The web page for the Dummies Press appears, as shown in **Figure 6-2**.

TIP

If you have trouble finding the address bar, try clicking with the mouse or tapping with your finger near the top of the screen, to the right of the three buttons (Back, Forward, Refresh). This will make the address bar appear.

3. Select a link on the page with a click or a tap. Where are the links? Just about everywhere. When you move the pointer over a link, it changes from an arrow to a hand — that's how you can tell where the links are.

Back button

Forward button

Add to Favorites

FIGURE 6-2

4. Select the back arrow (or press Alt+left arrow) to return to the preceding page. This arrow is located in the upper-left corner of the screen (refer to **Figure 6-2**). Select the back arrow to backtrack and revisit pages.

5. Select the forward arrow (or press Alt+right arrow) to move forward to the page you visited in Step 3. The forward arrow is next to the back arrow (refer to **Figure 6-2**). The browser remembers the pages you visit to make it easy to go forward and back.

TIP

To zoom in and make a web page look bigger, press Ctrl+plus sign. To zoom out, press Ctrl+minus sign.

6. Select the Add to Favorites or Reading List button in the upper-right corner of the screen. After you select this button, a panel appears, as shown in **Figure 6-3**. Select the Add button to add Dummies.com to your Favorites list. Later in this chapter, "Bookmark and Revisit Your Favorite Websites" explains how to go to your favorite websites by selecting sites on the Favorites list.

FIGURE 6-3

TIP

You can change the text in the Favorites panel before you select the Add button. However, there's usually no need to change the text unless it's overly long or unclear.

TIP

Browsing the web consists of entering addresses, following links, going forward and back, and revisiting your favorite websites. Relatively simple activities that can absorb hours.

7. Keep Edge open if you want to go on to the next topic in this chapter.

Open Multiple Pages in Separate Tabs

1. Open Edge if it isn't already open.

2. Go to the Google website at www.google.com. You can get there by typing www.google.com in the Address box and pressing Enter.

3. Select the New Tab button (or press Ctrl+T). This button is located to the right of the rightmost tab, as shown in **Figure 6-4. top**. The Where to Next? web page appears, as shown in **Figure 6-4, middle**. What's more, a new tab (not coincidentally called New Tab) appears at the top of the screen.

New tab

New tab button   **Switch between tabs**

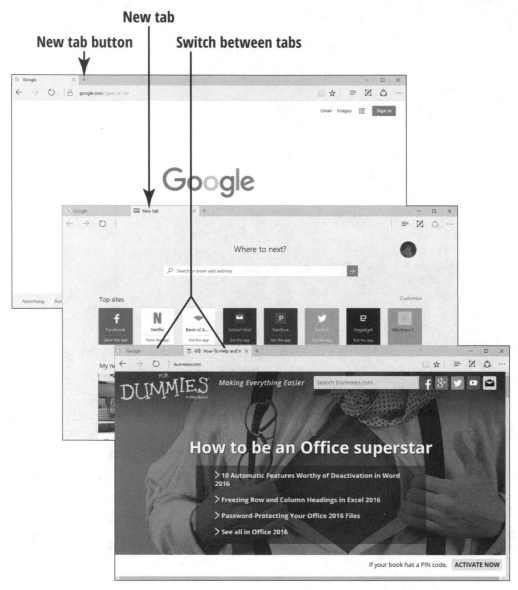

FIGURE 6-4

4. On the new tab, enter www.dummies.com in the address bar and press Enter. You open the Dummies website on the second tab, as shown in **Figure 6-4, bottom**. Now two websites are open in Edge. Google. com is open on the first tab; Dummies.com is open on the second. Notice the web page names on the tabs.

TIP

To close a tab, select its Close button (the X) or make sure that you are looking at the page you want to close and press Ctrl+W.

5. Select the first tab, the one with the name Google. You return to the Google website.

Browsing in multiple tabs allows you to keep one page open while visiting another, perhaps to compare information or to follow a different thought.

TIP

The keyboard shortcut for switching between tabs is Ctrl+Tab.

6. Select the X on the Dummies.com tab to close that particular tab. Close tabs when you want to reduce clutter and simplify switching between open tabs.

TIP

The keyboard shortcut for closing the current tab is Ctrl+W. (*W*? Long story.)

Search for Anything

1. With Edge open, select the address bar and then type **travel**. A list of websites with the word *travel* appears, as Edge attempts to match what you type with a page that you have browsed. (Ignore this list for this exercise, but take advantage of it later.) Select Bing Search on the right side of the address box or press Enter.

TIP

You can search the Internet from the Start screen without opening Edge. In the Search the Web and Windows box on the left side of the taskbar, type a search term. The Search panel lists items pertaining to the search term you entered, including ideas for web searches. Select a web-related item to search with Edge.

2. A search results page appears, as shown in **Figure 6-5**. The results come from www.bing.com, which is the default search engine for Edge. A *search engine* is simply a website that provides links to web pages that match your search. (That definition, however, ignores the complex process going on behind the scenes.)

3. Scroll down the page of search results. Select any link you want to follow. If you get to the bottom of the page, select Next to see more search results.

Search results and advertisements

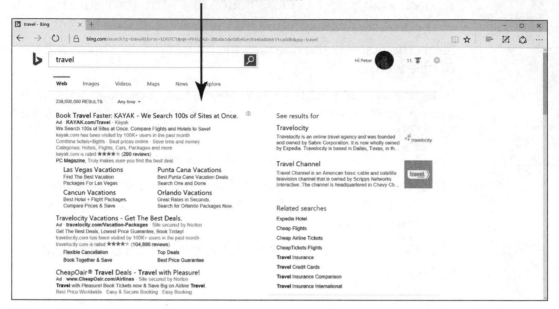

FIGURE 6-5

TIP

Some of the "search results" are advertisements. In Bing searches, the results at the top of the page and the right side of the page are paid for. Be careful of these advertisements, which are designed to sell you something, not to provide information. If you prefer not to see advertisements on web pages, see "Turn Off Ads on Web Pages" later in this chapter.

4. Return to the previous screen by selecting the back arrow (or pressing Alt+left arrow).

5. Select the address box and type **travel new mexico** (no capitals needed). As you type, potential matches for your terms appear in the drop-down list. If you see an item matching the search you want, select it in the list. Otherwise, press Enter.

TIP

Different search engines turn up different results. Other search engines include Google (www.google.com), Ask (www.ask.com), and Yahoo! (www.yahoo.com). To use one of these search engines when exploring the web, enter its address in the address box.

6. Note the tabs at the top of the Bing page, below the search box. The first tab is Web, which contains the results you see by default.

Additional tabs vary with the search. Select each of the tabs, which may include any of the following:

- **Images** displays pictures matching your terms.

- **Videos** displays clips and snippets related to your search terms.

- **Maps** will help you get there.

- **News** displays search results from recent news, instead of all the results of the broader web.

- **Explore** presents a hodgepodge of feature articles and articles about how to use Bing.

7. Leave Edge open if you want to move on to the next topic.

Bookmark and Revisit Your Favorite Websites

1. Open Edge, if it isn't already open, and go to your favorite website on the Internet (or if you don't have a personal favorite, go to mine: `www.google.com/advanced_search`). If you've spent any time on the Internet, you soon find websites that you want to visit again and again. Rather than memorize the addresses of these websites, you can add them to your Favorites list to make revisiting them quite easy.

2. Select the Add to Favorites or Reading List button (it's shaped like a star). The Favorites panel opens, as shown in **Figure 6-6**. Use this panel to describe the websites you want to revisit, and store their names in the Favorites panel (you'll take a look at the Favorites panel in Step 4).

3. Before selecting the Add button to add your favorite website to the Favorites list, consider doing the following:

- Enter a shorter, more concise, more descriptive name in the Name text box.

- Open the Save In menu and select a folder name to store the website in a folder. (Step 8 explains how to create folders of your own.)

FIGURE 6-6

4. To verify that the website you are currently visiting has been added to the Favorites list, select the Hub button, select the Favorites button in the Hub panel, and look for your website in the Favorites panel, as shown in **Figure 6-7**.

5. Select the Back button to go to the website you visited previously. This button is located in the upper-left corner of the screen. Next, select the Hub button and, in the list of bookmarked websites, select the website you bookmarked in Step 3 (see **Figure 6-7**). Your favorite website opens on the screen.

Don't hesitate to bookmark a website that you expect to revisit. Unless you bookmark it, you might not be able to find it again.

TIP

To remove a website from the Favorites list, display the Favorites list, move your finger or the pointer over the website's name, display the context menu, and select Remove.

TIP

6. The Favorites bar appears below the address box (I show you how to display it in Step 7). Merely by clicking or tapping a website name on the Favorites bar, you can go straight to a favorite website without having to open the Favorites panel. Go to a favorite website and select the Add to Favorites or Reading List button. The Favorites panel opens (refer to **Figure 6-3**). On the Save In menu, choose Favorites Bar and then select the Save button.

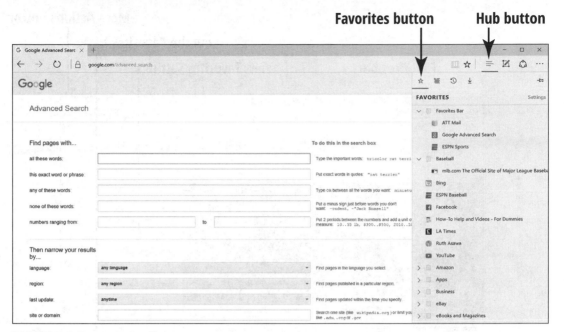

Favorites button   **Hub button**

FIGURE 6-7

7. To display the Favorites bar, select the More Actions button and choose Settings on the drop-down menu. In the Settings panel, select View Favorites Settings, and in the Favorites Bar panel, choose Show the Favorites Bar, as shown in **Figure 6-8**. Any website you really, really like is a candidate for the Favorites bar.

8. Select the Hub button and then select Favorites to open the Favorites panel (refer to **Figure 6-7**). From here, you can manage websites that you have deemed your favorites:

- **Reorder the websites and folders:** Drag a website or folder up or down in the Favorites panel until it lands in the right place.

- **Remove a website (or folder):** Display the folder or website's context menu (right-click or touch it with your finger). Then choose Delete.

- **Create a folder:** Display the context menu by right-clicking an existing folder or touching an existing folder. Then choose Create New Folder on the context menu, scroll to the bottom of the Favorites panel, and type the folder's name.

- **Rename a website (or folder):** Display the context menu, choose Rename, and enter a new name.

More Actions button

Show the Favorites bar

Favorites bar

View favorites settings

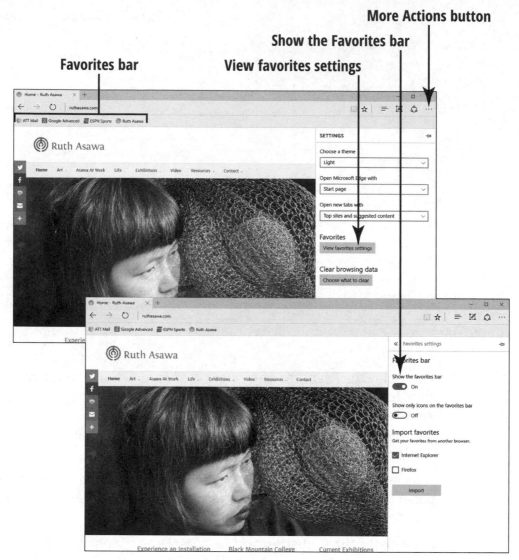

FIGURE 6-8

TIP

Folders can be a big help in organizing and finding bookmarks in the Favorites panel. If you're the type who likes to bookmark websites, give some thought to creating folders to store your bookmarks.

9. Leave Edge open if you want to move on to the next topic.

Explore Edge Features

1. Go to your absolute favorite web page so that you can pin this web page to the Start screen. Select the More Actions button (it's located in the upper-right corner of the screen). Then choose Pin to This Page to Start on the drop-down menu and select Yes in the confirmation dialog box that asks whether you really want to pin this web page to the Start menu.

2. Close Edge and then go to the Start screen and select your favorite web page's tile. By selecting this tile, you do two things at one time — you start Edge and open it to your favorite website. Isn't that convenient?

3. Select the Hub button, and in the panel, select the History button. As shown in **Figure 6-9,** the History panel opens. This panel offers the means to backtrack to websites you visited in the past hour, the past day, or the previous week.

4. Scroll to the bottom of the History panel to delve into ancient history and see websites you visited some time ago. Select a website to open it in Edge.

TIP

To erase your browsing history and remove all web page names from the History panel, select the Clear All History link (shown in **Figure 6-9**).

5. Steps 3 and 4 demonstrated how Edge keeps track of web pages you visited, but what if you resent this kind of snooping? You can browse the web without letting Edge keep a historical record of the websites you visited. To browse in private, select the More Actions button and choose New InPrivate Window in the drop-down menu. Edge opens a second, "InPrivate" window, as shown in **Figure 6-10**. Websites you visit privately are not recorded in the History panel. Close the InPrivate window for now (or browse a while and then close it).

TIP

You can tell when you're browsing privately because the word *InPrivate* appears in the upper-left corner of the Edge window (see **Figure 6-10**).

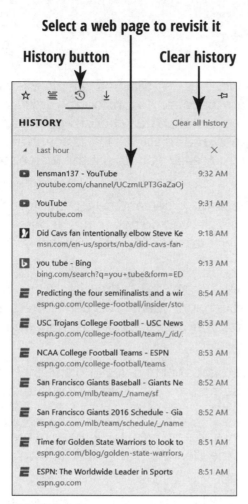

Select a web page to revisit it

History button   Clear history

FIGURE 6-9

6. When you start Edge, you see the start page, which offers websites and news stories that Microsoft thinks you will like (refer to **Figure 6-1**). You can, however, decide for yourself what you want to see when Edge starts. Select the More Actions button and choose Settings on the drop-down menu. The Settings panel opens, as shown in **Figure 6-11**. Under Open Edge With, tell Edge what you want to see first thing:

Private browsing notice

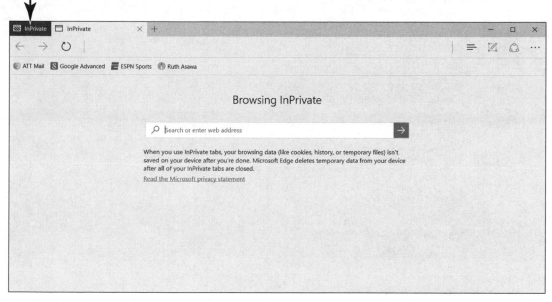

FIGURE 6-10

- **Start page:** Contains websites and news stories that Microsoft thinks you will like based on your browsing history (refer to **Figure 6-1**).

- **New tab page:** You see the Where to Next? page with an address box and links to popular websites (refer to **Figure 6-4**).

- **Previous pages:** You can see web pages that you were reviewing the last time you closed Edge.

- **A specific page or pages:** After you choose this option, enter the address of the web page you want to see and select the Save button. You can enter more than one web page to open more than one when you start Edge.

7. Close Edge or keep reading if you're inclined to find out how to turn off the ads on web pages.

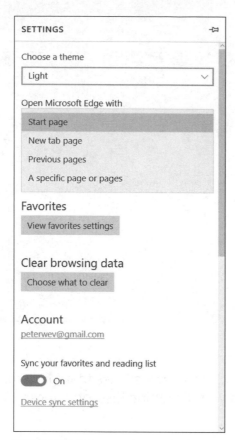

SETTINGS ⇥

Choose a theme

| Light | ⌄ |

Open Microsoft Edge with

Start page
New tab page
Previous pages
A specific page or pages

Favorites

View favorites settings

Clear browsing data

Choose what to clear

Account
peterwev@gmail.com

Sync your favorites and reading list

◉ On

Device sync settings

FIGURE 6-11

Work with the Reader App

1. Open Edge if it isn't already open.

2. Type `irs.gov/pub/irs-pdf/fw4.pdf` in the address box and press Enter. A U.S. government web page opens, showing a W-4 tax form. You can read this form in the Reader app after you download it.

TIP

If you see the message *Make Adobe Reader My Default PDF Application,* select Cancel. Adobe Acrobat Reader is a program often used to open these documents on computers other than Windows 10.

3. Save this PDF file to your computer with one of these methods:

- Right-click and choose Save As on the context menu.

- Hold your finger on the screen until Save As appears on the context menu.

4. In the Save As dialog box, save the file to the Downloads folder and select the Save button.

5. Open the Reader app and select Browse on the Reader screen. In the Open dialog box, go to the Downloads folder, select the fw4 file, and tap or click the Open button. The W-4 form opens in Reader, as shown in **Figure 6-14**.

TIP

If you don't see the Browse button, swipe from the bottom edge of the screen or right-click and then click or tap the Open Another File button (the plus sign). Next, choose Open File.

6. In Reader, select the app button in the upper-left corner of the screen and choose App Commands to display the app bar (shown in **Figure 6-12**).

7. Select the Two Pages button on the app bar to display two pages simultaneously. Select One Page to see just one page at a time. Continuous displays the largest size text and less than one page at a time.

8. In the Reader app bar, select Find, which enables you to search a document for text. Type **dependent** and then select the magnifying glass or press the Enter key. Every instance of matching text is highlighted. Select Next or Previous to move through the document. Select Results to display a list of matching items in context (useful for long documents). Select Close to end the search.

9. Display the app bar one more time and then select More, which displays the following functions:

- **Rotate** is useful if the document is not rotated correctly.

- **Info** displays information about the document, including who created it and when, as well as the document length. Permissions indicate what functions are available, with printing being the most important.

Display the app bar

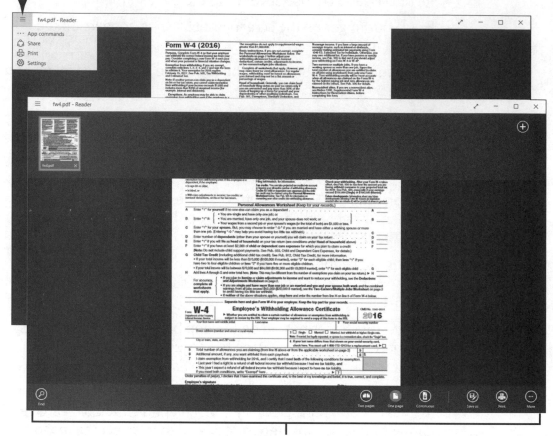

Reader app bar

FIGURE 6-12

10. To print this document, select Print. The Print dialog box opens. Select your printer and then select the Print button (or select Cancel). For information on installing (and using) a printer, see Chapter 13.

Some documents are quite long, requiring more than one page of paper. Be certain that you want to print.

TIP

11. Close the Reader app.

Chapter 7

Emailing Family and Friends

E mail has largely replaced the notes and letters of previous centuries. Every day, billions of email messages circle the globe, conveying greetings, news, jokes, even condolences.

Email also provides a way to send and receive *attachments*, such as documents or photos. Who needs faxes or postcards?

The Mail app gives you access to email using your Microsoft Account. Your Microsoft Account can be associated with an email address from any email service provider, including Microsoft's own Hotmail (`www.hotmail.com`), Live (`www.live.com`), Outlook (`www.outlook.com`), or Xbox (`www.xbox.com`). You can also use email services such as Yahoo! (`www.yahoo.com`) and Gmail (`www.gmail.com`) without having a Microsoft Account. However, you have to access non–Microsoft Account email using a web browser or an app other than Microsoft's Mail app. See Chapter 6 for information on browsing the web.

In this chapter, you use the Mail app for email. You compose, format, and send email, files, and pictures. You also discover how to respond to incoming email.

TIP If you don't have a physical keyboard, see Chapter 1 for information on using the virtual keyboard.

Use the Mail App

1. For email on Windows 10, select the Mail tile on the Start screen. The Mail app opens. If you're not currently signed in using a Microsoft Account, enter your email address and password on the Sign In screen that appears and then select Sign In. (See Chapter 4 for information on creating a Microsoft Account.)

TIP The first time you use the Mail app, you are invited to "add your accounts." In other words, Windows 10 offers its help linking an email account you have to the Mail app. Select the Add Account button and follow the onscreen instructions for making an email account available to the Mail app. See "Add an Email Account to Mail," later in this chapter, for more information.

2. When you start the Mail app, you land in the Inbox folder. If you haven't used your Microsoft Account for email, you probably don't have any messages in your Inbox folder. Who would have written you already? You may, however, see a message or two from Microsoft.

3. On the Inbox screen, select the Expand/Collapse button, as shown in **Figure 7-1**. The Folders panel expands and you can see the names of all your folders in the Folders panel. In the Mail app, email is kept in folders. The numbers beside the folder names tell you how many unread email messages are in each folder.

4. Select any of the following folders in the Folders panel and then select the Expand/Collapse button to return to the Mail panel (you have to select More in the Folders panel to see some of these folders):

    - **Outbox:** When you send email, it moves to the Outbox until it has been processed, which may be instantaneously. If you're not connected to the Internet, email waits here until you establish a connection, and then it is sent.

    - **Inbox:** Email you have received but not moved elsewhere appears here, including both read and unread email.

- **Archive:** The Mail app provides this folder for email that you want to keep on hand for archival purposes.

- **Drafts:** As you compose email (next section), you can save your message as a draft until you are ready to send it.

- **Junk:** Messages are moved here — either automatically or by you — instead of the Inbox, if they are suspected of being, well, *junk*. The more common term for unwanted email is *spam*. (It's a long story.) You may want to check this folder occasionally to see whether a message was misfiled here.

- **Sent:** Copies of the email you send are stored here, appropriately enough.

- **Trash:** Self-explanatory? You can move deleted messages out of the Trash folder if you change your mind about deleting them.

Select the Expand/Collapse button to expand the Folders panel

Select to conduct a search

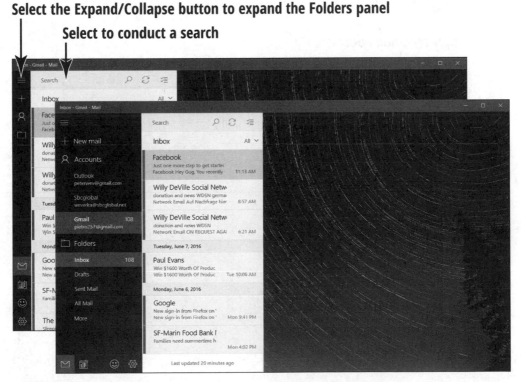

FIGURE 7-1

You may see other folders in the Folders panel besides the folders described here. If you linked the Mail app to an email account with other folders, those folders are also listed in the Folders panel.

5. Proceed to the next section, "Write an Email Message."

To search for stray email messages, go to the Search box, and enter the content you're searching for. For example, enter a subject, sender, or something in the message.

Write an Email Message

1. To compose an email message in the Mail app, select the New Mail button (it looks like a plus sign) in the upper-left corner of the screen. (It doesn't matter which folder you're in when you select this button.) The Compose screen appears, as shown in **Figure 7-2**.

Enter an email address

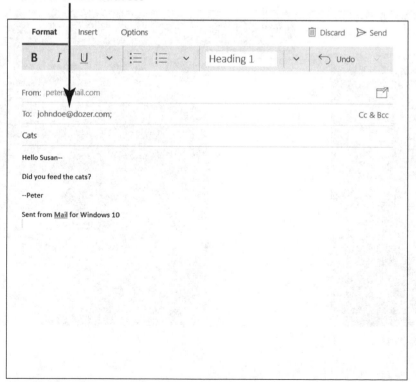

FIGURE 7-2

2. In the To box, type an email address. If the Mail app recognizes the address because you've sent email to or received email from the person to whom you're addressing your message, a pop-up box appears so that you can select the person's address without having to type it. Press the Tab key, touch the screen, or use the mouse to move to the next option.

To send email to more than one person at one time, select the Cc & Bcc button (located to the right of the address line). Then type a recipient's address in the Cc box (and the Bcc box as well, if you want to send a blind copy without revealing you've done so). (Once upon a time, *CC* stood for *carbon copy*, and then it became *courtesy copy*.) Technically, it makes no difference whether you use additional To addresses or the CC.

3. Enter a few words in the Subject box describing your message's content or purpose.

4. Select below the Subject line. Type your message. Avoid all caps — purists consider caps to be SHOUTING! No need to press Enter as you approach the end of the line — this isn't a typewriter.

Some people start a message with a salutation, such as *Hi Peter*, but many people do not. Some people sign email using their initials. Email can be as formal or casual as you choose to make it.

Words underlined with a red squiggle aren't recognized by Windows 10 and may be misspelled. Right-click or tap and hold to see a pop-up menu, and choose Proofing on the menu. You see a list of suggested spellings. Choose the correct spelling if it is on the list. You can also go to the Options tab and select the Spelling button there.

5. When you're ready to send the message, select the Send button (you'll find it in the upper-right corner of the Compose window). If you decide not to send the message, select the Discard button.

Email you compose but haven't sent yet is kept in the Drafts folder. You can postpone writing a message and finish it later by going to the Drafts folder and opening your message there. To go the Drafts folder, select the Expand/Collapse button (if necessary) and then select Drafts in the All Folders panel.

6. If you select the Send button, your message is sent and you return to the folder you were in at the beginning of Step 1.

7. Repeat from Step 1 as needed.

8. Mail puts a signature at the bottom of email messages: "Sent from Mail for Windows 10." If you don't like this signature or want to put your own signature at the bottom of all the emails you send, select the Settings button on the bottom of the Folders panel. The Settings panel opens. Select Signature and either turn off signatures or enter a signature of your own.

TIP

Format Email

1. If you want to add bold, italics, or other formats to email, select the text you want to fancy up in the Compose window, as shown in **Figure 7-3**. If no text is selected, your formatting will apply to the word in which the *cursor* (the blinking vertical line in the content) is located.

- **Mouse:** Click and drag the mouse pointer over the text you want to select.

- **Touchscreen:** Tap and drag over the text you want to select.

- **Keyboard:** With the cursor at the beginning of the text you want to select, hold down the Shift key as you press the right or down arrow to select text. Release the Shift key only after you have completed your selection.

To apply formatting to one word, double-click or double-tap that word to select it and display the app bar in one step.

TIP

The keyboard shortcut to select all text is Ctrl+A. No mouse or touchscreen method is quite so complete.

TIP

2. Using the commands on the Format tab, select from the following formatting options:

- **Bold:** Bold is used for emphasis to make text stand out.

- **Italic:** Although italic can also be used for emphasis, it may be harder to read than normal or bold text.

- **Underline:** Because links are usually underlined automatically, you may want to avoid underlining text that isn't a link.

Format the text

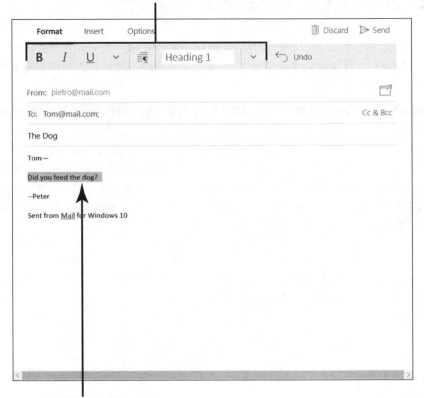

Select the text to format
FIGURE 7-3

- **List:** Select the Paragraph Formatting button and choose Bullets or Numbering on the drop-down menu to create a list.

- **Styles:** Choose a style from the drop-down menu. A style applies many formats simultaneously. Heading 1, for example, enlarges the text and turns it blue.

See Chapter 1 for information on using the virtual keyboard's emoticons.

To create a hyperlink, go to the Insert tab and select the Link button. Then enter the address destination of the hyperlink in the Address box that appears. See Chapter 6 for more information about hyperlinks.

3. When you finish formatting the text, select the Send button.

Send Files and Pictures

1. To send a file or picture with your email message, go to the Insert tab. As shown in **Figure 7-4**, the Insert tab offers tools for sending files and pictures.

2. Select the Files button to send a file. The Open dialog box appears. Locate and select the file you want to send and then select the Open button in the dialog box. You can send more than one file with an email message. In the Compose window, files you want to send appear as thumbnails under the heading "Attachments" (see **Figure 7-4**). Click the X button on a file if you change your mind about sending it.

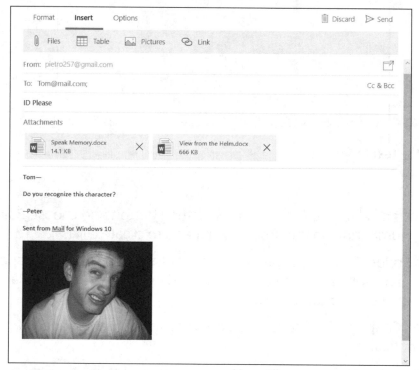

FIGURE 7-4

3. To send a picture with an email message, place the cursor where you want the picture to be. Then select the Pictures button on the Insert tab. The Open dialog box appears. Select the picture and then click or tap the Insert button.

TIP

You can format pictures before sending them. Click or tap a picture to select it in the Compose window. The Picture tab appears. Using the tools on this tab, you can rotate, crop, and resize pictures.

4. When you have finished attaching your files and pictures, select the Send button to send them on their merry way.

TIP

Chapter 10 explains how you can use the Photos to send photos to others.

Read and Respond to Incoming Email

1. On the Start screen, select the Mail tile. The Mail app opens to the Inbox folder.

2. Select a message under the Inbox heading. The content of that message appears to the right, as shown in **Figure 7-5**.

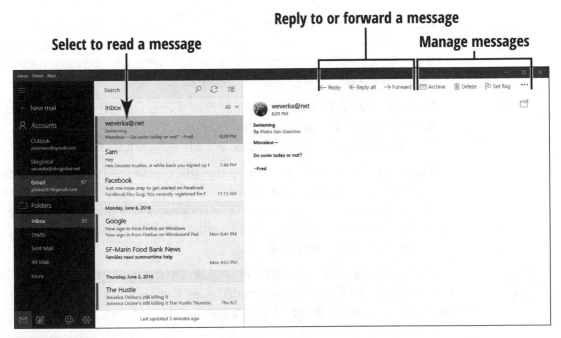

Select to read a message

Reply to or forward a message

Manage messages

FIGURE 7-5

3. After you read the message, you can respond to or forward it if you want. Select the Reply or Reply All button to reply; select the Forward button to forward the message. Selecting any of these buttons starts a new message (refer to **Figure 7-2**) that includes the text of the original message. The subject line is automatically *RE: [the original subject]* (in the case of replies) or *FW: [the original subject]* (in the case of forwarded messages). Complete your message and select the Send button.

Reply All sends your response to all the other recipients, if a message is addressed to more than one person. The Reply option sends your response only to the sender. Select Forward to send the selected message to someone else. You can add your own text or remove portions of the forwarded message in the process.

See the sections "Write an Email Message" and "Format Email," earlier in this chapter, for more information on composing an email message.

4. Select any message in the Inbox category. Note the following options for managing messages (to take advantage of some of these options, select the More button in the upper-right corner of the screen):

- **Delete:** Use this option to delete the message.

- **Set Flag:** Use this option to place a flag icon next to the message in the Inbox so that you remember to deal with the message later on. You can swipe right to flag a message.

- **Mark Unread/Read:** Use this option if you want the message to appear unread (marked with a horizontal blue line in the Inbox). Some people do this with messages they want to deal with later.

- **Move:** Use this option to move the selected email from one folder to another. To access the Move option, select the More button, the three dots on the right side of the toolbar. After you select Move on the More drop-down menu, select a folder in the Move To panel to move your email.

If you add email accounts from providers such as Gmail, you may see additional categories or options. See the section "Add an Email Account to Mail" at the end of the chapter.

Change Mail Settings

1. In Mail, display the Settings panel, shown in **Figure 7-6**. To display the Settings panel, display the Folder panel and select the Settings button (you'll find it in the lower-right corner of the Folder panel). The Settings panel appears on the right side of the Mail screen.

FIGURE 7-6

2. On the Accounts panel, select Manage Accounts, and then select the email account with settings that need a change. The Account Settings dialog box appears (see **Figure 7-7, left**).

3. Negotiate the Account Settings dialog box and select the Save button:

- **Password:** Enter the password of your email account here so that you don't have to enter it each time you collect email from the account.

- **Account Name:** The name of the email service provider. You can change this, if you want. I might use *Peter's email*.

- **Change Mailbox Sync Settings:** Click or tap here to open the Sync Settings dialog box (see **Figure 7-7, right**) and change how and when the Mail app collects email. Skip to Step 5 if you choose this option.

- **Delete Account:** Deletes the email account. The Mail app is no longer associated with the account after you delete it.

Enter a password

Change sync settings

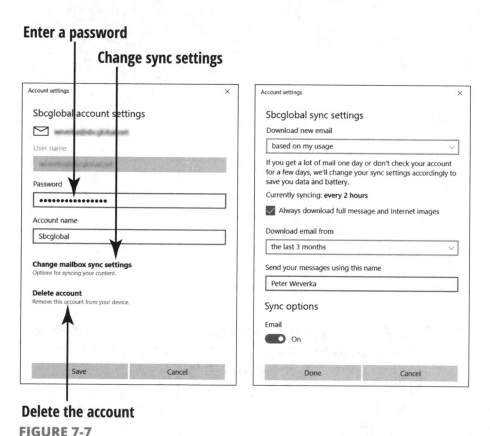

Delete the account

FIGURE 7-7

4. In the Sync Settings dialog box (see **Figure 7-7, right**), choose settings and select the Done button:

    - **Download New Email:** If you don't want email constantly streaming into your Inbox, you can change this setting to every 15 or 30 minutes, Hourly, or Daily.

    - **Download Email From:** You can limit how far back to download messages to your computer. This setting isn't relevant in a new email account.

    - **Send Your Messages Using This Name:** Enter the name under which you want your emails to be sent.

    - **Sync Options:** Turn this setting to Off only if you don't want to the Mail app to receive email from the account.

Add an Email Account to Mail

1. If you have another email address, you can add it to Mail. For example, follow these steps to add an existing Gmail account to Mail. In Mail, display the Settings panel (refer to **Figure 7-6**) and then select Manage Accounts.

2. In the Manage Accounts panel, select Add Account.

TIP

Many people have more than one email address. Your Internet service provider probably gave you an email account, and you may have another through work or school. However, this feature isn't for everyone.

3. In the Choose an Account dialog box, select the service with which you have an email account. If your service doesn't appear here, select Other Account. If you have a Gmail address (or you just want to see what's next), select Google.

4. On the Connecting to a Service screen, enter your Gmail address, select Next, and enter your password in the appropriate box. Then select Sign In. Select the Back button if you don't want to continue.

5. The next screen informs you how your Gmail account will connect with the Mail app. Scroll to the bottom of this screen and select the Allow button.

6. In the All Done screen, select the Done button. As shown in **Figure 7-8**, the Manage Folders panel shows you the names of your accounts. You can switch to a different account by selecting its name in the Folder panel.

TIP

See the preceding section, "Change Mail Settings," for the steps to review or change settings for your newly added account.

Switch among accounts

‹ Manage Accounts

Select an account to edit settings.

✉ Outlook
peterwev@mail.com

✉ Sbcglobal
weverka@s.net

✉ Gmail
pietro@mail.com

🔗 Link inboxes

＋ Add account

FIGURE 7-8

Chapter 8

Exploring Apps for Your Daily Life

This chapter describes a handful of apps that the average Joe or Jane might use every day. It shows how to store contact information — names, email addresses, phone numbers, and the like — in the People app so that you can find this information quickly. You also use the Calendar app to keep track of birthdays, anniversaries, appointments, and other events.

This chapter delves into the Maps app, showing you how to use it to get directions and to look up hotels and restaurants when you're on the go. You see how the News app can help you keep up to date with the news, and how you can track stocks and bonds with the Money app.

Finally, this chapter demonstrates how to make the Lock screen indicate whether you've received email.

Add Contacts to the People App

1. On the Start screen, select the People app.

2. If you haven't signed in already using your Microsoft Account, the Sign In screen appears. Enter your Microsoft Account email address and password, and then select Sign In.

TIP

You need a Microsoft Account to use Mail, Calendar, and People. When you sign in to one, you're signed in to all three apps. See Chapter 4 for information on creating a Microsoft Account.

3. What you see first in People depends on whether the app found contact information associated with your Microsoft Account. You may see familiar names or an invitation to connect to other services. For now, add one new contact manually. (You connect to other services later.) Display the New Contact screen by selecting the New Contact button, as shown in **Figure 8-1**.

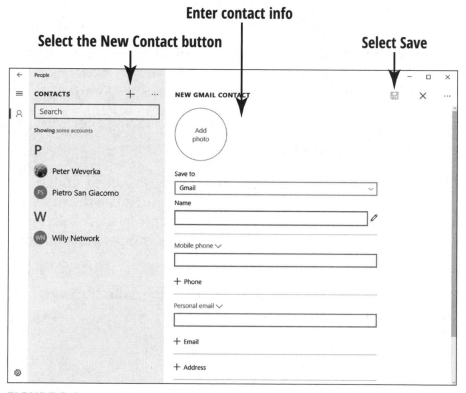

FIGURE 8-1

4. Much of the information on the New Contact screen (shown in **Figure 8-1**) is optional. Enter the information that you want access to throughout Windows 10, not just in the People app. (For example, think about what you want to access in Mail.) You can enter any person's name and information you want, but let me suggest the following:

   - **Save To:** Ultimately, you may link multiple accounts using the People app. Which account do you want this new contact associated with? For now, only one option may be available.

   - **Name:** Enter the contact's full name.

   - **Personal Email:** Select Personal Email and notice the three email categories — Personal, Work, and other — on the pop-up list. Choose a category and enter the contact's email address.

   - **Mobile Phone:** Select Mobile Phone and note the many categories of phone numbers — Home, Work Company, and so on — on the pop-up list.

5. Note the following buttons with plus signs. Select each in turn to see the available options. Add data as you please:

   - **Email:** Add up to two more email addresses.

   - **Phone:** Add up to seven more phone numbers!

   - **Address:** Add up to three mailing addresses.

   - **Other:** Options include Job Title, Significant Other, Website, and Notes, a box for free-form notes.

6. When you're done, select Save to add this contact (or select Cancel to throw away the new contact). The added contact appears on your list of contacts. Select the person's name to see his or her contact information, as shown in **Figure 8-2.**

TIP

Select the Edit button (it looks like a pencil) to edit a contact's information. After you select the Edit button, the Contact screen appears so that you can edit away.

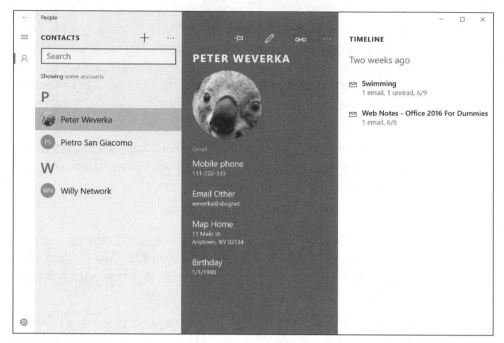

FIGURE 8-2

Delete a Contact

1. Open the People app if the People app isn't already open.

2. In the Contacts list on the left side of the screen, select the name of the contact you want to delete. Especially if your list of contacts is a lengthy one, it pays to go through the list from time to time and delete the names of people you are no longer associated with.

TIP

On the People screen, select a letter or type a name in the Search box. Selecting a letter scrolls the contact list to names with the letter you selected. After you type a name, press Enter to search. Matches appear on the left. Select the person whose contact details you want.

3. Select the More button, shown in **Figure 8-3**. Selecting this button opens a drop-down list.

4. Select Delete on the drop-down list.

5. In the dialog box that asks whether you really want to do it, select the Delete button (refer to **Figure 8-3**).

More button

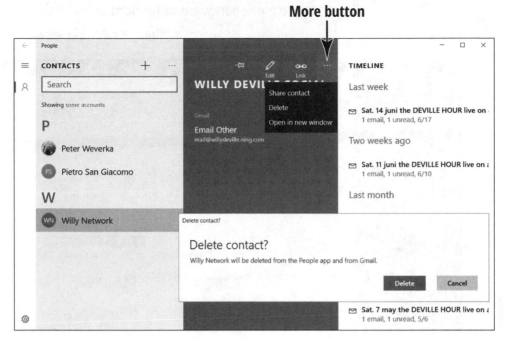

FIGURE 8-3

Add a Birthday or Anniversary to the Calendar

1. To see the calendar and add events, open the Calendar app from the Start screen, as shown in **Figure 8-4**. You may see events and appointments from services you connected to in People or Mail.

2. On the Calendar app bar located along the top of the screen (refer to **Figure 8-4**), select each of the following formats:

- **Day:** This format displays a single day with a box for each hour. Select arrows near the top of the screen to scroll back or forward one day at a time. Scroll up and down to see more hours in the day.

- **Work Week:** The current work week (Monday through Friday) appears. As with the Day format, scroll up and down to see different hours and use the arrows to move forward or back a week at a time.

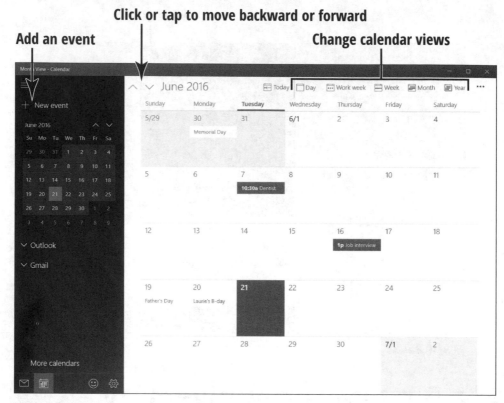

Add an event

Click or tap to move backward or forward

Change calendar views

FIGURE 8-4

- **Week:** The current week appears. Scroll or use the arrows to go from hour to hour or week to week.

- **Month:** The current month appears in the classic month layout. (Depending on the size of your screen, you may have to scroll to see this format.) Today is highlighted with a different color. Use arrows near the top to move forward and back a month at a time.

- **Year:** The months of the year appear. You can select a month to open a month in Month view.

TIP

Select the Today button on the Calendar app bar to go immediately to today's date on the Calendar.

3. The Calendar offers two ways to add an event, the short-but-cursory way and the slow-but-thorough way:

- **Short but cursory:** Click or tap the day on which the event is to occur (in the Month format) or the hour and date on which it is to occur (in the Day or Week formats). You see the pop-up window shown in **Figure 8-5**. With luck, this little window is all you need to describe the event. Type the event's name, and if it isn't an all-day event, deselect the All Day check box (if necessary) and use the start time and end time menus to describe when the event starts and ends. You can also type the event's location. Select the Done button when you finish describing the event (or select the More Details button to open the Details screen and go to Step 4).

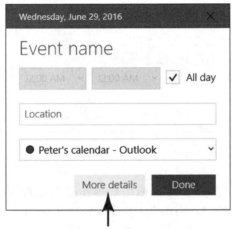

Open the Details screen

FIGURE 8-5

- **Slow but thorough:** Select the New Event button (refer to **Figure 8-4**). The Details screen appears, as shown in **Figure 8-6**. Move on to Step 4.

4. Under Details, enter or (or change) any of the following data for the event:

- **Event Name:** Describe the event in one to three words. The description you enter will appear on your calendar.

- **Location:** If listing the location will help you get to the event on time, by all means list it. The location, like the event name, appears on the calendar.

- **Start and End:** Select the calendar icon, and on the pop-up menu that appears, choose the day on which the event begins and then the day on which it ends.

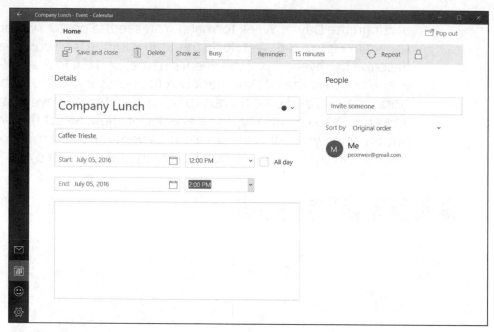

FIGURE 8-6

- **Hours/All Day:** If this isn't an all-day event, deselect the All Day check box, if necessary. Then use the drop-down menus to describe when the event will occur.

TIP

If the event is one that recurs, you can schedule it on a weekly, monthly, or yearly basis on the calendar. Weekly staff meetings, birthdays, and anniversaries are examples of recurring events. Select the Repeat button on the app bar along the top of the screen to schedule a recurring event. Then, using the Repeat options that appear in the Details screen, describe how often the event occurs, when it occurs, and when it will cease occurring.

- **Event Description:** Describe the event in detail if you think it's necessary. Should you wear the tux or zoot suit? The ball gown or the formal dress? This is the place to record your thoughts on the matter.

5. Optionally, use the commands on the app bar at the top of the screen to further describe the event:

- **Show As:** Choose an option on this menu if you share your calendar with someone, such as a receptionist, who may schedule you for other events. You can declare yourself free, tentative, busy, or out of the office.

- **Reminder:** How far in advance of the event do you want Calendar to display a notification? Choose None, 5 Minutes, 15 Minutes, 30 Minutes, 1 Hour, 1 12 Hours, 1 Day, or 1 Week.

- **Private:** Select this option to prevent this event from appearing on a shared or public calendar. The event remains visible on your own screen.

6. When you're done, select the Save and Close button. (Select the Delete button if you don't want to create an event.)

7. On the calendar, your event appears on the specified date and time.

8. To edit an event, select it on the calendar. The Details screen opens. Add or change any detail.

TIP

To delete an event, open it in the Details screen and select the Delete button select the Delete button (a trash can).

Search and Explore with the Maps App

1. Select the Maps app on the Start menu to open the Maps app. Use this app to locate places and to get driving or walking directions.

2. Click or tap in the Search box. A drop-down list appears, as shown in **Figure 8-7**. It lists items you already searched for, if you searched already. You can select an item on the list to revisit it.

3. Type **de young museum** in the Search box. As you type, options appear in the Search panel. Select the de Young Museum in San Francisco. As shown in **Figure 8-7**, the Maps app shows you where the de Young Museum is located; it also provides some information about the museum.

4. Select the Zoom Out button (or press Ctrl+minus sign) on the app bar in the map. Then select the Zoom In button (or press Ctrl+plus sign). The tools on the app bar can help you read the map better (refer to **Figure 8-7**).

Enter a search term

Zoom in and out

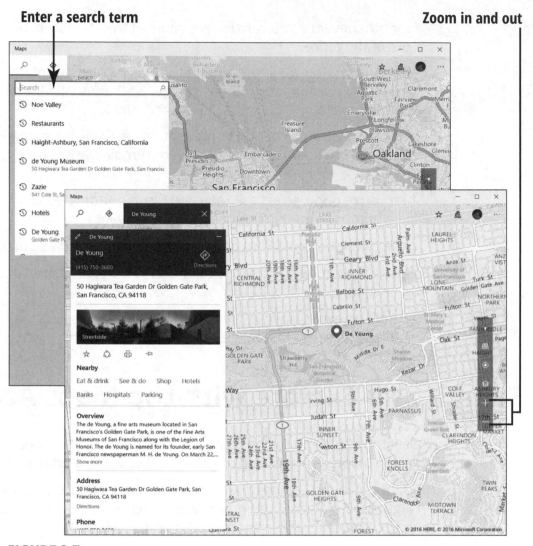

FIGURE 8-7

5. In the Search panel, select Directions. In the From box, type **haight-ashbury** and then select Haight-Ashbury, San Francisco, California in the search results. The Maps app gives you driving directions between the two locations and tells you how long the drive will take. Rather than enter a search term, you can enter street addresses if you know the address of the place you want to go.

6. Are you walking, not driving? In that case, select the Walking icon at the top of the Search panel to get directions for walking between the two locations.

7. Select the Search button (the magnifying glass in the upper-left corner of the screen) and then select Restaurants in the drop-down list that appears. You see a list of restaurants on the map, as shown in **Figure 8-8**. You can select the name of a restaurant to find out more about it. You can select the word *Directions* under a restaurant name to get directions for going there.

Close the Restaurant list

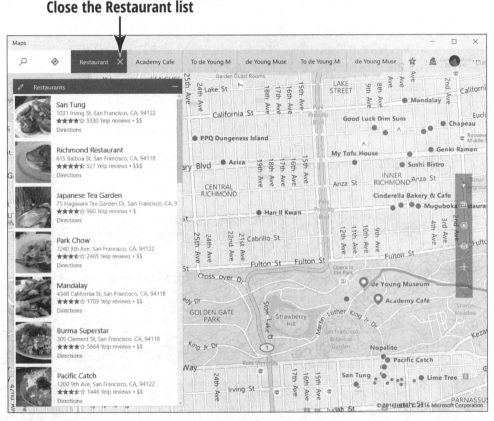

FIGURE 8-8

8. Select the Close button (the X) on the Restaurant tab to close the restaurant list (refer to **Figure 8-8**). The Maps app keeps tabs on your travels. Select a tab along the top of the screen to retrace your steps and revisit a map you saw earlier.

Get the Latest News with the News App

1. Open the Start menu, and click or tap the News app tile to open the News app. Use this app to get the latest news about topics of interest to you. The first time you open this app, it offers you the chance to "personalize your news." In other words, you get the chance to tell the News app which topics interest you. Select Skip for now. Later I'll show you how to declare your favorite news topics.

2. As shown in **Figure 8-9**, you can select an area of interest — Top Stories, World, Crime, and so on — on the menu bar along the top of the screen to steer your search for news in a different direction. Select World on the menu bar to look for world news.

Personalize the news   **Go to an area of interest**

FIGURE 8-9

3. Select the Interests button (the star) in the menu bar along the left side of the screen. You see the Interests screen shown in **Figure 8-10**. This is where you select the type of news you want the App to deliver to your computer screen.

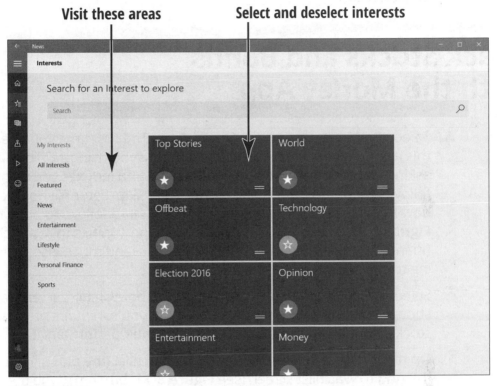

Visit these areas   **Select and deselect interests**

FIGURE 8-10

4. Visit the Interests screens and deselect or select the topics you want for the menu bar along the top of the News app (refer to **Figure 8-9**). To select or deselect a topic, click or tap its star. For example, deselect Technology on the My Interests screen if you don't care to get news about technology; select Golf on the Sports screen if you want Golf to appear as a topic on the menu bar.

5. Select the Sources button in the menu bar along the left side of the screen to open the Sources screen. This is where you tell the News app where to get your news. Select Sports, for example, to go to the Sports screen and choose sources for your sports news. The choices include ESPN and NBA.com.

6. Select the Local button in the menu bar along the left side of the screen to tell the News app where you live. This way, the News app can update you with the local news.

7. Close the News app (or linger a while longer and catch up on the latest news).

Track Stocks and Bonds with the Money App

1. Select the Money app on the Start screen. The first time you open this app, you get the chance to "personalize your money." The app is asking you to declare which stocks, bonds, and indexes you want to follow. Ignore this offer for now and select Skip. Later I'll show you how to state what kind of financials you want to follow. As shown in **Figure 8-11, top**, the Money app offers opportunities to research financial markets, investment opportunities, and much else pertaining to the root of all evil.

2. Select Watchlist on the menu bar to open the Watchlist screen, as shown in **Figure 8-11, middle**. From here, you can maintain a list of stocks, bonds, and mutual funds to track their performance.

3. On the Watchlist screen, select Add to Watchlist (the plus sign). On the Add to Watchlist screen (see **Figure 8-11, bottom**), type the ticker symbol or name of the security you want to track, and then select an option from the list that appears. The stock, bond, or fund you select is added to the watchlist, and you return to the Watchlist screen.

4. To investigate the performance of a security, select its name in the Watchlist (select the name of the security you're most interested in). A screen similar to the one in **Figure 8-12** opens. From here, you can take a hard look at the security to see whether it's worth keeping or investing in.

5. Select the Pin to Start button. Selecting this button places a tile for this security on the Start screen. Open the Start screen now and look for the security you just "pinned." You can click the security's tile to open Money to the screen where the security's performance is

tracked. Pin a security to the Start screen when you're keen to know how it's performing.

TIP

To remove a security from the Start screen, return to the screen in Money where it is tracked and select the Unpin from Start button.

Add a security

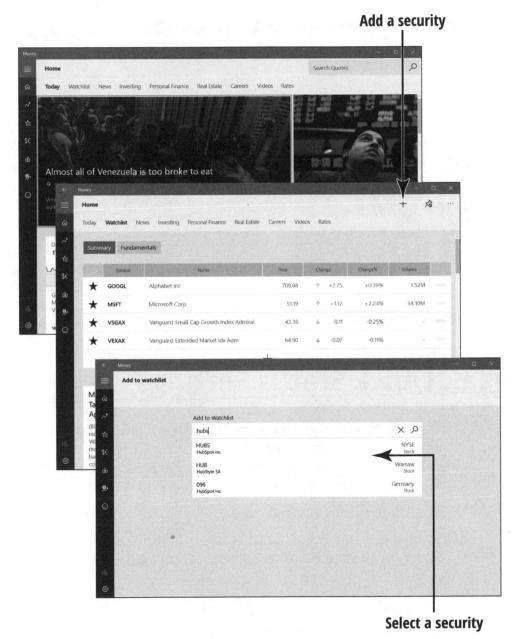

Select a security

FIGURE 8-11

CHAPTER 8 **Exploring Apps for Your Daily Life**   155

Pin to Start

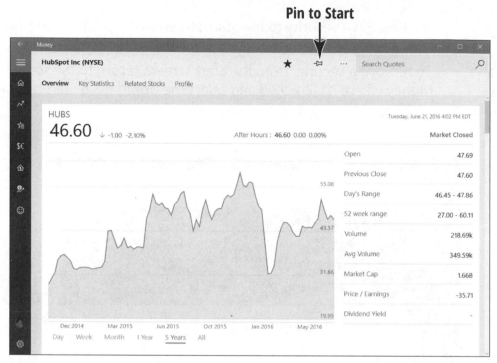

FIGURE 8-12

6. Close the Money app (or rummage around a while longer to see what else it has to offer).

Tweak Quick Status Settings

1. Quick Status settings appear on the Lock screen to show you what's what. To change these settings, open the Start screen and select Settings. On the Settings screen, select Personalization. On the Personalization screen, select Lock Screen.

TIP

See Chapter 3 for information about the Lock screen settings.

2. Scroll to the bottom of the Lock screen settings to the Choose Apps to Show Quick Status item, as shown in **Figure 8-13**.

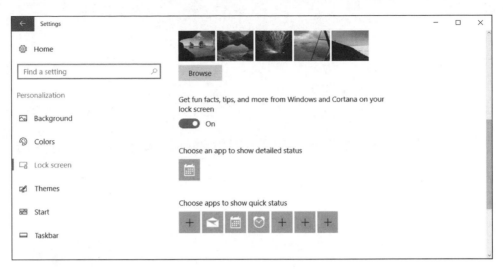

FIGURE 8-13

3. Some apps can display quick status information on the Lock screen. For example, Mail displays the number of unread messages in the Mail app. To add an app to the Lock screen, select one of the plus signs and choose an app name on the pop-up menu.

4. To change one of the current apps, select its icon and then choose a different app on the pop-up menu.

5. To remove an app from the Lock screen, select it and choose None on the pop-up menu.

6. Return to the Start screen.

3

Having Fun with Windows 10

Chapter 9

Exploring the Microsoft Store

You can do many things with Windows 10, such as send email, browse the web, play games, and look at photos and videos. You can read the news and chat with family and friends. All these functions and more involve computer programs. Back in the day, such programs were called *applications.* Now, we call them *apps.*

Windows 10 comes with a few apps installed, such as the Weather and Money apps. (See Chapter 2 for information on using these two apps and apps in general.) To obtain other apps — free or otherwise — you use the Microsoft Store.

To install an app from the Microsoft Store, you need a Microsoft Account. See Chapter 4 for information on setting up a Microsoft Account.

Microsoft tests and approves all apps in the Microsoft Store. For quality and security reasons, you can install Windows 10 apps only from the Microsoft Store.

In this chapter, you peruse the apps and games in the Microsoft Store, including those already installed on a new machine. You install a new game, discover how to manage the apps and games you own, and see how to rate and review an app or game. Finally, you find out how to make sure that the Microsoft Store can receive payments in case you want to buy an app or game.

Explore Apps and Games by Category

1. On the Start screen, select the Store tile.

2. Look over the Store home screen, as shown in **Figure 9-1**. The home screen shows top-rated and free apps and games, as well as apps and games that Microsoft thinks you will be interested in based on your previous purchases, if you made any. Notice the navigation bar along the top of the screen (see **Figure 9-1**). It offers five choices: Home, Apps, Games, Music, and Movies & TV. Wherever your travels take you in the Store, the navigation bar appears along the top of the screen so that you can return to the home screen or redirect your search for apps, games, music, or movies and TV shows.

Navigation bar

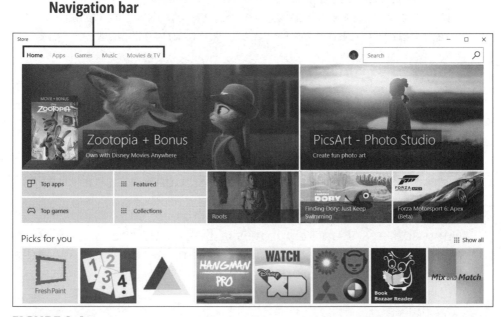

FIGURE 9-1

TIP

You can also navigate in the Store by selecting the Back button in the upper-left corner of the screen. Selecting this button returns you to the previous screen you were looking at.

3. Select Apps on the navigation bar to go to the Apps screen, and then scroll toward the bottom of the screen. As you scroll downward, you see the familiar categories — apps that Microsoft recommends for you, essential apps, top free apps, best-rated apps, and so on. If the apps in a category interest you, you can select the category's Show All button to investigate the apps in the category.

4. At the bottom of the Apps screen, you see the categories shown in **Figure 9-2.** Now you're getting somewhere. These categories are very useful for finding apps that are worth installing on your computer. Using the scroll bar as necessary, take a moment to look over the app categories:

Select a category to start browsing

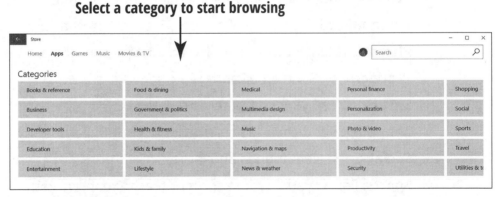

FIGURE 9-2

- **Books & Reference:** Read and research.

- **Business:** Analyze business data.

- **Developer Tools:** Make your software work better.

- **Education:** Study the stars, languages, or piano, or prep for the SAT.

- **Entertainment:** Check out apps that don't fit the other categories, such as those for drawing.

- **Food & Dining:** Locate eateries, as well as rate and review restaurants.

- **Government & Politics:** Learn more about the government and its workings.

- **Health & Fitness:** Want to get in shape? There's an app for that.

- **Kids & Family:** Discover family-activity apps and apps for children.

- **Lifestyle:** If you think entertainment is a vaguely defined category, check out lifestyle.

- **Medical:** Get medical information.

- **Multimedia Design:** Be creative with photos and video.

- **Navigation & Maps:** Get there faster.

- **News & Weather:** Keep current.

- **Personal Finance:** Track your spending and investing.

- **Personalization:** A catchall category if ever there was one.

- **Photo & Video:** View, edit, and share photos and videos.

- **Productivity:** Send email and create schedules.

- **Security:** Keep your computer and data safe.

- **Shopping:** Put the world's catalogues at your fingertips.

- **Social:** Connect to friends and family.

- **Sports:** Follow your favorite sport or team. (Yeah, cricket!)

- **Travel:** Get you there and back.

- **Utilities & Tools:** Check out apps for your computer.

You may see other categories, as well.

TIP

Is the app you want educational or entertainment? Will it make you productive or is it a tool? The category to which an app is assigned is determined by the app developer. In some cases, it's not clear why an app is in one category and not another. So it goes.

5. Select the Education category. In the Refine list on the left side of the screen, select Top Free to see apps you can install for free (see **Figure 9-3**). Then select Best-Rated to see apps that users have given the highest ratings. The Refine options are there to help you find apps. They are available wherever you travel in the Store app.

Refine your search

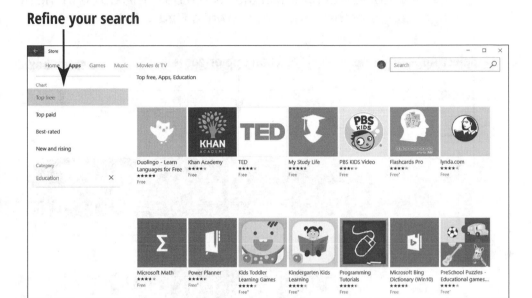

FIGURE 9-3

6. Select Games on the navigation bar and scroll to the bottom of the Games screen. You pass the familiar "top-rated" and "top free" categories. On the bottom of the screen are categories you can select to browse by category. The Games screen works just like the App screen.

7. Return to the Store home screen using one of these methods:

- **Back button:** Click or tap the Back button as many times as necessary to return to the home screen. This button is located in the upper-left corner of the screen.

- **Navigation bar:** Select Home on the navigation bar (refer to **Figure 9-1**).

Did you see an app you want to acquire as you completed these steps? If so, skip to "Install a New App or Game," later in this chapter.

TIP

Search for an App or Game by Name

1. On any Store screen, click in the Search box. This box is in the upper-right corner of the screen, as shown in **Figure 9-4**.

Select Apps or Games   Select an app or game   Search box

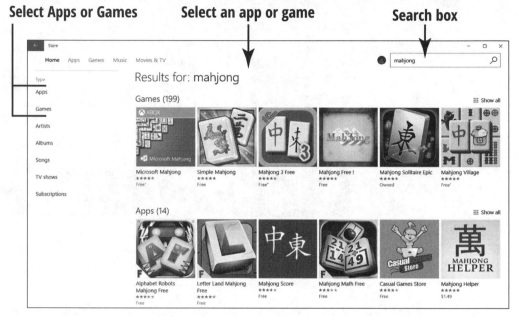

FIGURE 9-4

2. Type *mahjong* in the Search box and press Enter. As shown in **Figure 9-4**, apps and games with the word *mahjong* in their names appear in the Results window. (If you scroll to the bottom of the Results window, you'll see albums and songs pertaining to mahjong as well. Who would expect that?) The Results screen tells you how many apps and games match your search. After this initial search, you can turn the search in different directions:

- **Refine the search:** Select Apps or Games in the Refine list to narrow the search results to apps or games.

- **Show all apps or games:** Select a Show All link to see only apps or games on the screen.

3. Select Games in the Refine list to see games with *mahjong* in their titles, as shown in **Figure 9-5**. Notice that the Refine list has changed. Now you can select a category in the Refine list to narrow the search results to games in a particular category.

FIGURE 9-5

4. Scroll to Mahjong Free in the search results. Then select this game on the Results screen, as shown in **Figure 9-5**.

5. Proceed to the next section, "Install a New App or Game," or return to the home screen.

Install a New App or Game

1. In the Store, display the Mahjong Free screen. (See the section "Search for an App or Game by Name" for details.)

2. The screen shown in **Figure 9-6** appears. This (and any) game or app screen has lots of information.

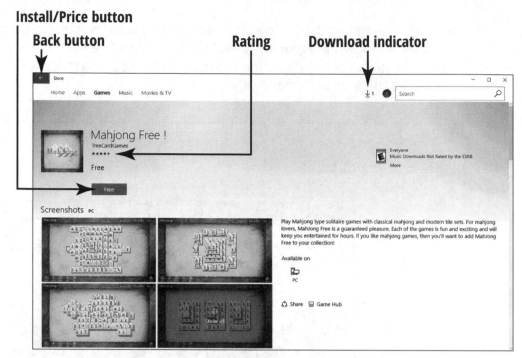

Install/Price button

Back button   **Rating**   **Download indicator**

FIGURE 9-6

TIP

> The Back button (left-pointing arrow) next to the game's name takes you back to the previously viewed screen.

3. On the top half of the screen, note the following:

- The Install/Price button (don't click it just yet), which lists the cost of the app or game

- The average rating in stars (five stars is the best)

- A description of the app or game

  For more details about the app or game, select the More link below the description.

- Screenshots that show what the app or game looks like onscreen

4. To read reviews by users, scroll down. You see the reviews that Microsoft deems most useful.

5. For additional information, including the age rating and the game or app's category, scroll down to the bottom of the screen.

6. Select the Install/Price button (refer to **Figure 9-6**) to download and install Mahjong Deluxe Free. Because the game costs nothing, the button reads "Free."

7. If you're not already signed in, enter your Microsoft Account email address and password on the screen that pops up. Then select Sign In.

TIP Many apps are free. Before you buy an app, see the section "Add Billing Information to Microsoft Store."

TIP If you purchase an app, you are buying a license to install that app on up to five machines using the same Microsoft Account. The Microsoft Store will track how many times and on which machine the app is installed.

8. The download indicator appears in the upper-right corner of the screen (refer to **Figure 9-6**) and a progress bar shows the game being downloaded and installed. When the installation is complete, *Mahjong Free was just installed. Check it out* appears below the description of the game or app.

TIP Installing an app may take a few seconds or a few minutes. You can do anything while an app installs — except use the app.

TIP If you don't see *Mahjong Free was just installed. Check it out,* the app may still be installing. If after a few minutes you still don't see this message, select the Install/Price button again.

TIP 9. To play Mahjong Free or to use any game or app after you install it, select the Start button. You may see the recently installed app on the Start menu under Recently Added, as shown in **Figure 9-7**. If you don't see it there, start your game or app the conventional way — by looking for the game or app in the alphabetical list (refer to **Figure 9-7**). If you haven't used an app yet, the word New appears below its name, as shown in the figure. Select the game or app's tile on the Start menu to open the game or app.

TIP You can move the Mahjong Deluxe tile to the Start screen. See Chapter 3 for information on rearranging tiles on the Start screen.

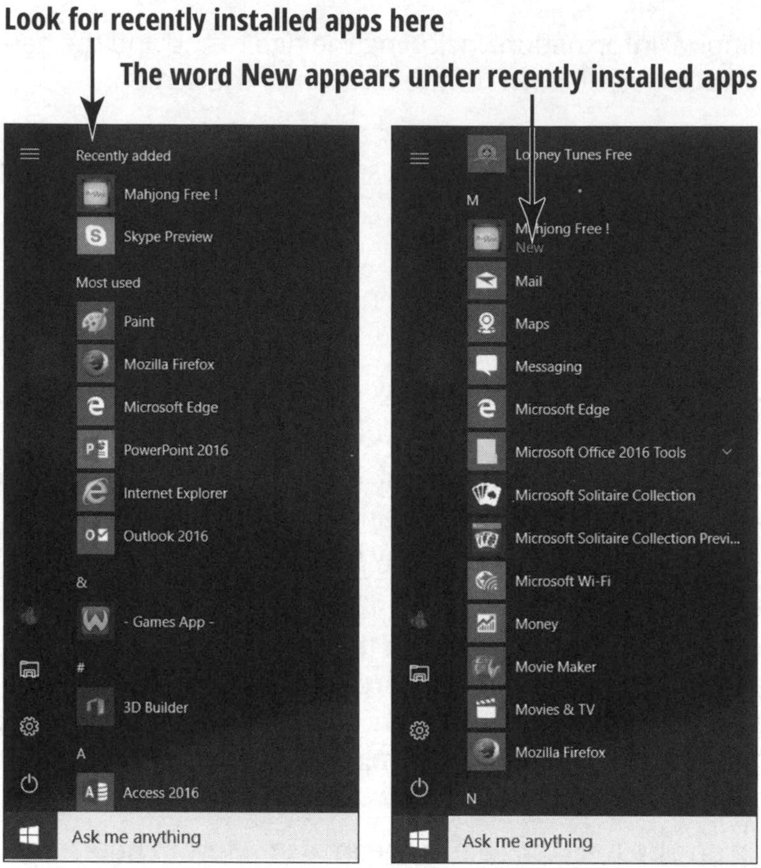

Look for recently installed apps here

The word New appears under recently installed apps

Recently added
- Mahjong Free !
- Skype Preview

Most used
- Paint
- Mozilla Firefox
- Microsoft Edge
- PowerPoint 2016
- Internet Explorer
- Outlook 2016

&
- - Games App -

#
- 3D Builder

A
- Access 2016

Ask me anything

- Looney Tunes Free

M
- Mahjong Free !
  New
- Mail
- Maps
- Messaging
- Microsoft Edge
- Microsoft Office 2016 Tools
- Microsoft Solitaire Collection
- Microsoft Solitaire Collection Previ...
- Microsoft Wi-Fi
- Money
- Movie Maker
- Movies & TV
- Mozilla Firefox

N

Ask me anything

FIGURE 9-7

Examine Your Apps and Games

1. To see which apps and games you have, select the User button. This button is located to the left of the Search box, as shown in **Figure 9-8**. A drop-down menu appears after you select the User button. This drop-down menu is the place to start when examining, updating, rating, and uninstalling apps and games.

2. Choose My Library on the User drop-down menu (refer to **Figure 9-8**). The Library screen appears, as shown in **Figure 9-9**.

3. Scroll to see which apps you have or select a Show All link to open a window that lists only your apps or your games. For each game or app, you see an icon, the name of the game or app, and its purchase date (even for free apps and games). Last, a downward-pointing arrow indicates whether the app or game has been successfully installed. If you don't see this arrow, the app or game isn't installed on your computer.

User button

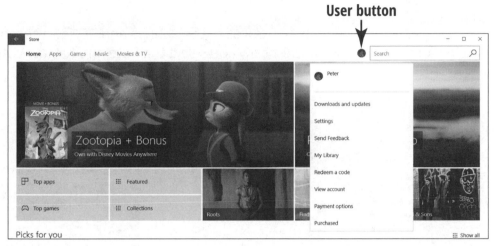

FIGURE 9-8

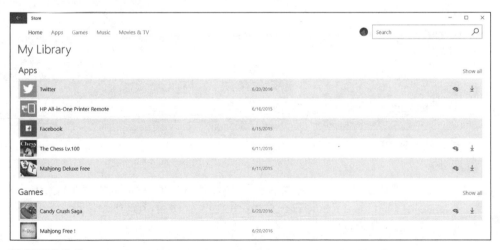

FIGURE 9-9

TIP

How can you have an app or game you haven't installed? If you sign into more than one computer using your Microsoft Account, you might install an app or game on one machine but not another.

Rate and Review an App or Game

1. On the Library screen (refer to **Figure 9-9**), select the Mahjong Free app. If you don't have this app, see the section "Install a New App or Game," earlier in this chapter, or substitute any app you have installed.

2. As shown in **Figure 9-10,** scroll to the Ratings and Reviews section of the Mahjong Free window and select the Rate and Review button. The Write a Review screen appears (refer to **Figure 9-10**).

FIGURE 9-10

TIP

Every app and game has a Rate and Review option. You can also select Write a Review on the details screen for that app in the Microsoft Store.

TIP

You can rate or review only apps and games that you've installed, and you must be signed in with your Microsoft Account. To rate or review a preinstalled app or game, install the app or game to associate the app with your Microsoft Account.

3. In the Rate This App menu, choose the number of stars you want to give this game. (Select one star for the lowest rating; select five for the highest rating.) In the Headline box, type a summary or overview of your comments, such as *Great app* or *Needs work*.

4. In the Tell Us box, say what you will, up to 500 characters, including spaces and punctuation. Be helpful, if possible. Select the Submit button when you're done with your review (or Cancel to abandon your review).

Your comments may help another person decide whether to install an app. In addition, the app's developer may use customer feedback to fix problems or add features.

Your Microsoft Account name and picture, if you have one — but not your email address — appear with your review.

Add Billing Information to Microsoft Store

1. To add the billing information necessary to buy apps, select the User button (refer to **Figure 9-8**) and select Purchased on the drop-down menu. Your browser opens to your Microsoft Account and you land on the Payment & Billing page.

See Chapter 4 for information on creating a Microsoft Account.

2. Scroll through the screen to make sure that the information here is accurate. If you are not being billed to the correct credit card or you want to change the credit card to which you are billed, select Payment & Billing on the toolbar and choose Payment Options on the drop-down menu that appears.

3. For security purposes, Microsoft asks you to enter your password on the next screen. Enter your password and select the Sign In button.

You may be asked on the next screen to verify who you are by submitting a security code. Provide the necessary information for Microsoft to contact you and select the Send Code button. After the code arrives by email or in a text message, enter it in the screen that asks for a security code.

4. Select a payment method (or select Edit Info if Microsoft already has credit card information on you) and do the following:

TIP

- Select your credit card type.

  You must fill out all parts of this form except for Address Line 2.

- Enter your credit card number in the box provided. Don't enter dashes or spaces.

- Under Expiration Date, select the month (MM) and year (YYYY) your card expires.

- Enter your name as it appears on your credit card.

- Under CVV, enter the three- or four-digit verification code from your credit card. (Select What's This? for an illustration of the location of this code on your card.)

5. In the Billing Address section, do the following:

- Enter your street address, city, state, and ZIP code.

- Select your Country/region.

- Under Phone Number, enter your area code in the first box and the remainder of your number in the second box.

6. When you're ready to continue, select Next.

7. If any of your data is incomplete or invalid, the form remains onscreen. Look for indications of a problem. Review each entry before selecting Submit.

8. If your information was accepted, you return to the Your Account screen. Under Payment and billing info, note your credit card type, the last four digits of your number, and the expiration date.

Chapter 10

Taking Photos and More

Windows 10 makes enjoying digital photos easy. You can pick and choose photos to look at or display a group of photos in a slide show. You set a favorite photo to be your Lock screen background so that you see it every time you start Windows 10. In this chapter, you see how to do all these things.

If you have a printer, you can print photos for yourself or to send to someone. Even black-and-white prints of color photos may be nice.

Of course, if you want to take your own photos, nothing beats having a digital camera. Copy photos from your camera to your Pictures folder for viewing and sharing. Or use the Camera app with the built-in camera found in many laptops and tablets.

In this chapter, you use the tools that come with Windows 10 for working with, sharing, and editing photos. You may want the additional features of a digital photo organizer and editing program. If so, check out *Digital Photography For Seniors For Dummies,* by Mark Justice Hinton (John Wiley & Sons, Inc.) for detailed steps on organizing, editing, and printing photos as well as on using a digital camera.

Take Photos (and Videos) with Your Computer

1. Select the Camera app on the Start screen. If you don't have a webcam, the app screen displays *Please connect a camera.* If you don't have a built-in webcam, or the resolution of the one you have is too low, you can easily add a webcam. Simply plug the camera into your computer — it's that easy.

TIP

You can choose from many good webcam models. Generally, get the highest video resolution you can afford, because you'll probably use the camera for video chats. Consider the size of the camera, its attachment to your computer, and whether it has a microphone (you definitely need a microphone).

TIP

For instructions about opening apps such as the Camera app, visit Chapter 2.

2. The first time you use the Camera app, the screen displays *Let Windows camera access your location?* Select Yes to continue. (If you don't want to continue, don't choose No unless you never expect to use this app. Instead, simply switch back to the Windows desktop.)

3. The Camera app opens, and there's a good chance you recognize the face staring back at you. Very likely the face isn't wearing dark glasses like the debonair guy in **Figure 10-1.** To take a photo, smile and then click or tap the Camera button. You may hear a shutter click. Your photo is placed automatically in a folder called Camera Roll in the Pictures folder.

4. If you see a Change Camera option, select that option. Some tablets and laptops have two cameras, one that faces you and one that points in the opposite direction. Switch to the camera away from you when you want to use your computer for something other than a self-portrait. Take another picture — they're free. Select Change Camera again to switch back to see yourself.

5. Select the Settings button located in the upper-right corner of the Camera window (shown in **Figure 10-1**). A panel appears with two options: Photo Timer and Settings. Select Photo Timer. The Phone Timer panel opens. Choose a Delay option — 2, 5, or 10 seconds — to

pause before photos are taken, and then select the check mark at the bottom of the window. You return to the Camera screen. Select the Camera button (shown in **Figure 10-1**) to take another photo. A countdown timer appears, giving you a few seconds to compose yourself. To turn off this feature, return to the Photo Timer panel and select the X button (not the check mark).

6. Select the Video button (shown in **Figure 10-1**). Nothing happens until you click or tap the button a second time, at which point you're in moving pictures. A counter indicates the length of the video. Short is sweet in video. You can speak, too. Click or tap the Video button to stop the video. As with photos you take with the Camera app, videos are saved initially in the Camera Roll subfolder of the Pictures folder. Select the Video button again to turn off the video function and return to taking still photos (with the next click or tap).

Leave the Camera app open to explore the Camera settings, which I explain next.

Start a video

Open the Photos app   **Choose Camera app settings**

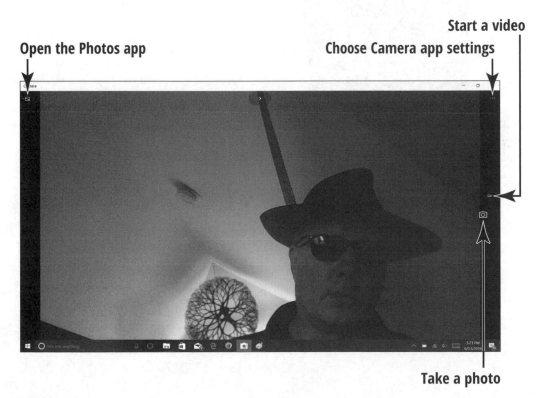

Take a photo

FIGURE 10-1

Choose Camera Settings

1. If the Camera app isn't open, open it now. Then select the Settings button located in the upper-right corner of the Camera window (refer to **Figure 10-1**). A panel appears with two options, Photo and Settings.

2. Choose Settings. The Settings panel opens, as shown in **Figure 10-2**. From here, you can tell the Camera app how to take photos and videos.

FIGURE 10-2

3. Under Press and Hold Camera Button, choose what happens when you hold down the Camera button rather than click or tap it. The Video option creates a video; the Photo Burst option creates a series of snapshots; the Disabled option turns this feature off.

4. Under Photos, decide how you want to take photos:

- **Aspect ratio:** These options determine whether you shoot narrow (the 4:3 option) or widescreen (the 16:9 option) photos.

- **Framing grid:** These options help you aim the camera. For example, the Crosshairs option places crossing lines in the center of the screen so that you know where the center of your photos will be.

5. Under Videos, decide how you want to take videos:

- **Video recording:** These options determine how many pixels appear in your videos across the screen horizontally and vertically. A *pixel* is one point of color. Suffice it to say, the more pixels in the setting, the larger the video screen is.

- **Flicker reduction:** These options reduce the flickering that can occur when video is taken under fluorescent light. Consider choosing an option other than Disabled if you are filming indoors. The 50 Hz (hertz) setting applies to the U.S. and Canada, where the AC (alternating electrical current) runs at 50 Hz; the 60 Hz setting applies to rest of the world.

6. Return to the Camera app by clicking or tapping the Camera app screen.

7. Return to the Start screen. See the section "View Photos" to see and maybe edit the photos you just took.

Copy Photos from Your Camera

1. If your digital camera came with a cable, connect that cable to the camera, connect the other end of the cable to a USB port on your computer, and turn your camera on. If your laptop or tablet has a built-in card slot, you can take the memory card out of the camera and insert it in that slot.

TIP

2. If your computer doesn't have a built-in card slot, consider buying a small memory card reader that plugs into your computer and works with your camera's memory card. You don't need a multicard reader, just a reader with a single slot the size of your camera card. I consider a card reader more convenient than using a cable.

TIP

The techniques described here for importing photos from a camera also apply to videos. Follow these steps as well to copy videos from your digital camera to your computer.

3. Windows 10 detects your camera and may briefly display a notification indicating *Select to choose what happens with this device.* If you're quick enough to tap or click this notification, Windows 10 displays your choices, as shown in **Figure 10-3.** Select Open Device to View Files, if that option is available, to open File Explorer to the photos on your camera, as shown in **Figure 10-4 (top)**. Then skip to Step 4. If you didn't catch the notification in time or you didn't see the notification, continue to Step 3 to import photos another way.

FIGURE 10-3

TIP

See Chapter 3 for information on increasing the time a notification remains onscreen.

4. Select the File Explorer icon on the taskbar to start File Explorer. Then look for and select your camera in the Folders panel on the left side of the screen (refer to **Figure 10-4, top**). Your camera is located under *This PC* in the Folder pane.

TIP

See Chapter 14 for detailed information about using File Explorer.

Select your camera (or one of its subfolders)

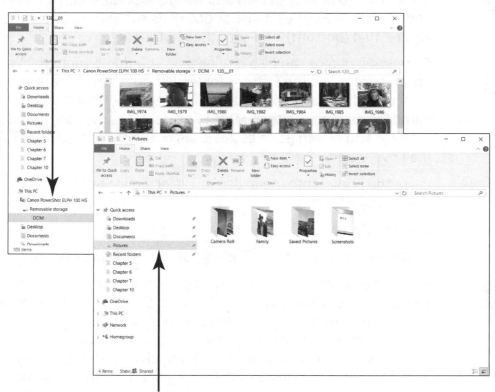

Copy to the Pictures folder (or one of its subfolders)

FIGURE 10-4

5. In File Explorer, select the photos you want to copy from your camera to your computer. Depending on your camera setup, the photos may be in a subfolder (refer to **Figure 10-4, top**). Use these techniques to select the photos:

   • Hold down the Ctrl button and click or tap photos to select them individually.

   • Press Ctrl+A to select all the photos in a folder.

6. Copy the photos you selected so that you can paste them into a folder on your computer. Use one of these techniques to copy the photos:

   • Press Ctrl+C.

   • On the Home tab in File Explorer, select the Copy button.

7. In File Explorer, select the folder where you want to copy your photos.

TIP

If you want to be able to view and edit your photos with the Photos app, select the Pictures folder or one of its subfolders, as shown in **Figure 10-4 (bottom)**, and copy the photos there.

TIP

Organizing photos can be a challenge. If you dump more than a few dozen photos into the Pictures folder without using folders, finding a specific photo later will be difficult. Using folders with unintelligible names doesn't help, either. Most of my folder names are based on the year and month (such as 2015–06) or the subject, such as Luke the Lovehound.

8. Paste the photos into the folder you selected in Step 6. Use one of these techniques:

- Press Ctrl+V.

- On the Home tab in File Explorer, select the Paste button.

TIP

If you often import photos from a digital camera or memory card, you can speed the process by telling Windows to open File Explorer immediately when you attach your camera or memory card to your computer. On the Start menu, choose Settings and type **autoplay** in the Find a Setting box. In the Search Results panel, select AutoPlay Settings. The AutoPlay window opens, as shown in **Figure 10-5.** In the Memory Card and Camera sections, choose Open Folder to View Files (File Explorer).

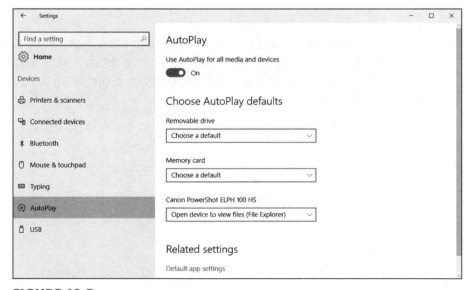

FIGURE 10-5

View Photos with the Photos App

1. To see photos on your computer, select the Photos app on the Start screen. The Photos screen opens to the Collection window, as shown in **Figure 10-6.** It shows the contents of the Pictures folder (and its subfolders) on your computer. Your screen will look different.

FIGURE 10-6

2. If you don't see any pictures, skip to one of the following sections:

- If you have a digital camera, see "Copy Photos from Your Camera."

- If your computer has a built-in camera or a webcam, see "Take Photos with Your Computer."

TIP

The Photos app shows photos you keep on OneDrive. To decide for yourself whether to show photos from OneDrive, select the Settings button. The Settings window opens. Turn off the Show My Cloud-Only Content from OneDrive option. Chapter 15 explains OneDrive.

3. If you see pictures, scroll down to see more photos. Photos are presented by the dates on which they were taken.

TIP

You can take a screenshot — a picture of the current screen — by pressing ⊞+Print Screen. (A touchscreen or mouse equivalent is not available.) The screen dims slightly to indicate the capture, which is stored automatically in the Screenshots folder in your Pictures folder. Use this technique to create your own documentation of problems or something you want to see again later.

TIP

4. Select any photo to display it in the Photos app window, as shown in **Figure 10-7**. Scroll through the photos by selecting an arrow on the left side (to go back) or right side (to go forward) of the screen or by clicking or tapping the right edge or left edge of the screen. You can also press the PageDown key (forward) or PageUp key (back).

5. Click or tap anywhere on your photo to display the app bar (see **Figure 10-7).** Select the Slide Show button. The photos appear in succession. Stop the slide show by clicking or tapping a photo.

TIP

Select the More button on the right side of the app bar to see names on the buttons. Selecting this button also displays some new commands — Open With, Copy, Print, Set As, and File Info. By selecting File Info, you can see each photo's name, when it was taken, and its file size.

6. Zoom in and out on a photo using one of these methods (repeat to zoom in or out more):

   • **Mouse:** Click the plus sign in the lower-right corner to zoom in. Click the minus sign to zoom out.

   • **Touchscreen:** Touch two fingers on the screen. Move your fingers apart to zoom in. Pinch your fingers closer together to zoom out.

   • **Keyboard:** Press Ctrl+plus sign (actually, press the equals sign — no need to press the Shift key) to zoom in. Press Ctrl+minus sign to zoom out.

TIP

Zoom in to see part of a photo made larger.

Use the Delete button in the app bar to delete a photo. See Chapter 14 for information on undeleting files.

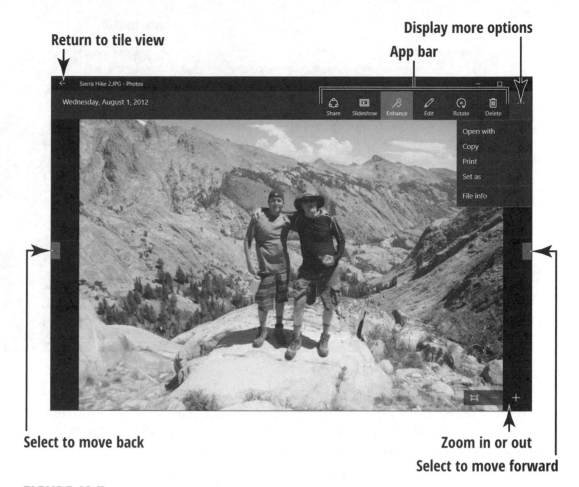

Return to tile view

Display more options

App bar

Sierra Hike 2.JPG - Photos

Wednesday, August 1, 2012

Share Slideshow Enhance Edit Rotate Delete

Open with
Copy
Print
Set as

File info

Select to move back

Zoom in or out

Select to move forward

FIGURE 10-7

7. Select the arrow on the left side of the app bar to return to tile view. In this view, you can see more than one photo.

The Photos app offers many options for editing photos. See the section "Edit Photos Using the Photos App," later in this chapter.

TIP

Share Photos by Email

1. In the Photos app, select one or more of your photos. To select a photo, tap or click it. You can tell when a photo is selected because a checkmark appears in its upper-right corner, as shown in **Figure 10-8**.

Share button

FIGURE 10-8

2. Click or tap the Share button to display the Share panel (refer to **Figure 10-8**). The Mail app icon and the number of selected photos appear in the Share panel.

   • On the Share panel, select the Mail tile.

   You can share using any apps that appear in the Share panel.

TIP

3. The Mail panel slides in from the right. Enter an email address under To. Add a subject. Thumbnail images of the photos you want to share appear in the content area. You can add a message below the photo. When you're ready, select the Send button in the upper-right corner.

   Chapter 7 explains the Mail app in details.

TIP

Print Photos Using the Photos App

1. In the Photos app, select one photo using a click or tap to display the photo at full screen.

2. Select the More button on the right side of the app bar (refer to **Figure 10-7**).

3. Select Print. The Print window appears, as shown in **Figure 10-9**. Select your printer.

FIGURE 10-9

TIP

If you have a printer but it doesn't appear in the list, you may not have selected a photo or you may have two or more photos selected. The Photos app doesn't have an option for printing more than one photo at a time.

4. Select a printer. Note the preview. Select the Print button.

TIP

Here's a handy keyboard shortcut that works in any app: Press Ctrl+P to open the Print window straightaway.

Edit Photos Using the Photos App

1. You can use the Photos app to change a photo, including making it smaller. In the Photos app, click or tap one photo for full-screen viewing. The right side of the app bar offers tools for editing photos: Enhance, Edit, and Rotate.

TIP

Sometimes when you import photos from a digital camera or scanner, they arrive askew because the photographer turned the camera the wrong way when shooting. You can correct this error by selecting the Rotate button. Selecting this button turns the photo by 90 degrees. Keep selecting the button until the photo turns right-side-up.

TIP

Selecting the Enhance button in the Photos app touches up your photos automatically. To see what your photo looks like when it is auto-enhanced, select the Enhance button.

2. Select the Edit button on the app bar (or press Ctrl+E). The Editing window opens, as shown in **Figure 10-10**. This window offers many tools for touching up photos. To edit a photo, select a retouching method on the left side of the screen and then choose options on the right side. For example, when you select Light on the left side of the screen, the right side offers commands for changing the Brightness, Contrast, Highlights, and Shadows in your photo.

3. Many photos can be improved by *cropping,* which involves cutting out distracting elements and keeping just part of the photo. You might crop a photo to concentrate on its most important part. To crop, make sure that the Basic Fixes method is selected on the left side of the screen and then select the Crop button. A box appears on the photo to indicate which parts will remain after cropping, as shown in **Figure 10-11**. To adjust the crop area, drag a corner of the box. As well, you can drag the photo itself to adjust the photo's placement.

TIP

Selecting the right area can be awkward. To start over, select the Cancel button or press Esc.

4. Select Apply. The selected area is all that remains, as shown in **Figure 10-12**. If you crop a very small area, you may want to zoom in to see the results.

TIP

You can undo each step by selecting the Undo button.

Choose an editing method

Choose options and settings

Save your edits

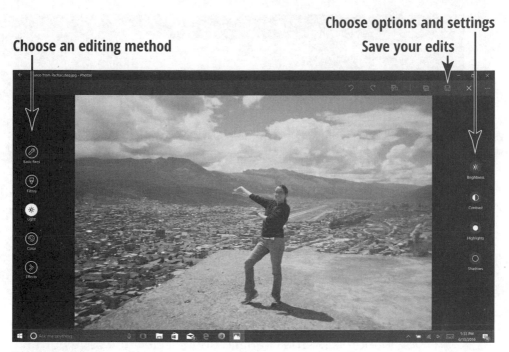

FIGURE 10-10

Select Apply

Adjust the size of the box to determine what is cropped

FIGURE 10-11

FIGURE 10-12

5. If you want to save the changed photo, select the Save button.

6. Besides cropping photos on this screen, you can adjust the brightness and color of your photograph, as well as apply special effects. Select Light, for example, and you can adjust the brightness and contrast.

7. Using the Filters method, you can take advantage of preset edits to photographs. After you select the Filters, filter presets appear on the right side of the screen. They offer the chance to change the light and color of a photograph in one fell swoop. Select the last preset, for example, to change your photo to black and white. Select Update Original if you want to save the edits you made to a photograph; press Esc or select Cancel if you decide not to keep your edits.

TIP

Photo Gallery is a great tool for viewing, organizing, editing, and printing photos. Search the Store for the latest photo apps. See Chapter 12 for information on installing Photo Gallery.

Chapter 11
Enjoying Music and Videos

The term *media* on computers refers to something other than text. Audio and video are examples of media. *Audio* is a catchall term for music and other sound files, such as books on CD. *Video* includes files you can shoot with your digital camera as well as Hollywood blockbusters.

The delivery of music has come a long way from Edison's wax cylinder or even vinyl LPs. Nowadays, music is entirely digital. The Groove Music app lets you play your music collection and makes it easy to explore new music. Use Windows Media Player to play audio CDs, to copy audio files to your computer, and to burn songs onto a CD.

The Movies & TV app is similar to the Music app, but is for video instead of music. You can use either app to buy new media as well as play what you have.

In this chapter, you play a CD, copy CDs to your computer for easier access, and burn a CD. You also explore the Groove Music and Movies & TV apps.

TIP

You'll need a different app to play DVDs. Search Microsoft Store for Media Center or for a DVD player app. See Chapter 9 for more information on Microsoft Store.

TIP

Popular alternatives for music or videos include Hulu, iTunes, Netflix, and YouTube. All these are accessible through the web browser. Search Microsoft Store for related apps.

Play and Copy Music from a CD

1. If you have a CD or DVD disc drive or slot on your computer, insert a music CD, label side up for horizontal drives. (Vertical drives are less predictable.)

2. Windows 10 detects your CD and may briefly display a notification indicating *Select what happens with audio CDs*. (You can also click the notification.) If you're quick enough to tap or click the first notification, Windows 10 displays your choices, as shown in **Figure 11-1.** Select Windows Media Player and then skip to Step 5.

FIGURE 11-1

TIP

See Chapter 3 for information on increasing the time a notification remains onscreen.

3. If you missed the notification, go to the desktop and select the File Explorer icon (which looks like a folder) in the taskbar.

4. On the left side of File Explorer, select This PC and then select the drive below Local Disk C:. You may see the words *Audio CD* or *DVD Drive*.

5. On the Ribbon, select the Manage tab under Drive Tools. Then select AutoPlay. As shown in Figure 11-1, the notification from Step 1 reappears (and stays onscreen until you select something). Select Windows Media Player, unless the Music app is available, in which case select the Music app and skip to the next section.

6. If you see the Welcome to Windows Media Player screen, select Recommended Settings and then select Finish. The Windows Media Player plays your music. Switch back to the Windows desktop. The music continues to play.

TIP

Don't confuse Windows Media Player with another Microsoft app called simply Media Player. Media Player is for playing audio, not copying audio files or burning audio files onto CDs.

7. For access to more options, select Switch to Library, a small button under the X in Windows Media Player, as shown in **Figure 11-2.**

FIGURE 11-2

8. Note the following controls at the bottom of the Windows Media Player, as shown in **Figure 11-3**:

Control music playback   **Switch to Now Playing**

FIGURE 11-3

- **Shuffle:** Select this button to turn on *shuffle,* which randomly mixes the tracks you play. Select again to turn off shuffle, and the tracks play in the order in which they appear onscreen.

- **Repeat:** Select this button to play all the tracks again after all have played. Select again to turn off the repeat function.

- **Stop:** Select to stop playing.

- **Previous:** Select this button to skip to the previous track. Select and hold to rewind to an earlier point in the track.

- **Play/Pause:** Select the button with two vertical lines to pause play mid-track. Select the same button (now with a triangle pointing to the right) to resume playing from the point you paused.

- **Next:** Select this button to skip to the next track. Select and hold to fast-forward through the track.

- **Mute/Unmute:** Select this button to silence the player. Although the track continues to play, you won't hear it. When Mute is on, a red circle with a slash appears next to the speaker icon. Select the button again to hear the track.

- **Volume:** Drag the slider to the left to decrease or to the right to increase the volume of the track. Your speakers may also have a manual volume control. Windows 10 has a separate volume control in the taskbar, as well.

- **Now Playing:** You select this button, which is located far to the right of the toolbar, to reduce the player to a small size (refer to **Figure 11-2**).

9. To copy the CD tracks to your Music library, select Rip CD.

Be sure to refer to this as *ripping a CD* around your younger friends. But not the youngest, because they think CDs are way passé and MP3s rule. (MP3 is an audio file format common to portable digital music players and music downloads.)

If you plan torip a lot of CDs, select Rip Settings ⇨ Rip CD Automatically and Rip Settings ⇨ Eject CD After Ripping. Just inserting the CD will copy files to your Music library as it plays the CD. Audiophiles should choose Rip Settings ⇨ Audio Quality ⇨ 192 Kbps (Best Quality).

10. When the copying process finishes, remove your CD. To play this music in the future, start Windows Media Player and choose Artist, Album, or Genre under Music. You can also play anything in the Music library using the Music app. See the next section, "Listen to the Music App."

Pin the Windows Media Player to the taskbar for easy access: Click the right mouse button over the icon in the taskbar, or tap and hold until a box appears and then release. On the menu that pops up, select Pin This Program to Taskbar. You can also search for Windows Media Player on the Start screen. See Chapter 2 for information on pinning apps to the Start screen.

If your music CD doesn't play automatically the next time you insert one, you can tell Windows 10 how to handle audio CDs. On the Start screen, click or tap Settings and then type **autoplay** on the Settings screen. In the search results, select AutoPlay Settings. The Settings screen opens to the AutoPlay settings. Turn the Use AutoPlay for All Media and Devices option on to make CDs play automatically.

Listen to the Groove Music App

1. Select the Groove Music app on the Start screen. The Groove Music app home screen appears, as shown in **Figure 11-4.** The Music app enables you to play songs that you ripped (copied) from CDs, songs that you purchased from iTunes and other music purveyors, and playlists that you created from songs you own.

TIP

If you see *Can't sign in*, you're not connected through a Microsoft Account. You'll still be able to do the steps in this section, though. You need to sign in only to buy music.

2. Initially, the Music app recognizes music files kept in these folders on your computer: C:\Users\Your Name\OneDrive\Music and C:\Users*Your Name*\Music. Maybe you keep your music files in other folders. To tell the Music app where your music files are, tap or click the Show Menu button to display menu options and select the Settings button (refer to **Figure 11-4**). In the Settings screen, select the *Choose Where We Look for Music* link. The Build Your Collection dialog box appears, as shown in **Figure 11-5**. Select the Add Folder button, choose a folder in the Select Folder dialog box, and tap or click the Add This Folder to Music button. Then select Done. Repeat these instructions to add all the folders where you store music files.

3. To find the song you want to hear, click the Show Menu button to display search options (refer to **Figure 11-4**). Now you're getting somewhere. Choose an option to conduct your search and select any search result for the next step:

   - **Search:** Type the name of an artist, album, or song in the Search box. As you type, suggested matches appear below the Search box. For now, ignore these suggestions (but take advantage of them in the future to save typing). Instead, select the magnifying glass or press Enter. Search results appear.

   - **Your Groove:** A list of albums you played recently appears. Scroll to find an album.

   - **Albums:** A list of albums appears. Scroll to find an album.

Show Menu button

Locate songs

Settings button

Filter and sort search results   **Play songs**

FIGURE 11-4

- **Artists:** A list of artists appears. Scroll to find an artist and select the artist's name to view his or her songs.

- **Songs:** A list of songs appears. Scroll to find a song.

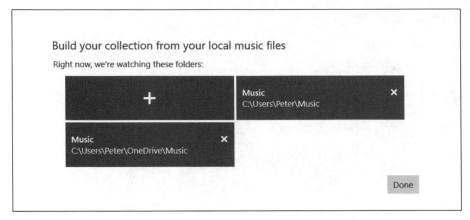

Build your collection from your local music files

Right now, we're watching these folders:

+

Music
C:\Users\Peter\Music ✕

Music
C:\Users\Peter\OneDrive\Music ✕

Done

FIGURE 11-5

TIP

If the search results list is a long one, you can narrow your search with the Filter and Sort options (refer to **Figure 11-4**). Filtering narrows the search results to songs on your computer, songs on OneDrive, and other criteria. Sorting arranges the results in alphabetical order, date-added order, or by genre, artist, or album.

4. Select a song or album in the search results. Note the following options (not all of which may appear on the current screen):

- **Play:** Plays the song. Notice the controls at the bottom of the screen for pausing the song and controlling the volume (refer to **Figure 11-4**).

- **Play (Album):** Plays the songs on the album, starting with song 1.

- **Add To:** Opens a pop-up menu with playlists, and you can add the song to one of those playlists (see "Create and Manage Playlists," the next topic in this chapter).

- **Explorer Artist:** Opens a screen with other songs you own by the same artist. Click the back arrow to return to the Results screen.

TIP

You can listen to music as you conduct a search. To return to the song or album that is currently playing, select the Now Playing button.

5. Check the volume level on your speakers. Tablets and laptops often have physical volume controls — look around the edges. To adjust volume levels using Windows 10, select the Speakers icon on the right side of the taskbar. A volume slider appears, as shown in **Figure 11-6**.

Slide the control to adjust the volume. Select the speaker icon on the right side of the slider to mute or unmute all sounds. Select anywhere in the Music app to dismiss the volume slider.

FIGURE 11-6

6. Switch back to the Start screen. The Groove Music app continues to play. The Groove Music tile on the Start screen displays the album art and title of the current song. Select the Music tile to return to the app.

7. Leave the Groove Music app open if you care to discover how to create a playlist, the next topic in this chapter.

Create and Manage Playlists

1. Create a playlist with the Groove Music app to play your favorite songs — songs from different artists — one after the other. After you create the list, you select it in the Groove Music app to play it. To create a playlist in the Groove Music app, select the Create New Playlist button (a plus sign). You see the Name This Playlist dialog box, shown in **Figure 11-7**. Enter a descriptive name for your playlist and select Save.

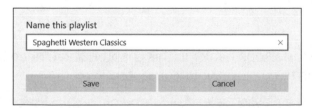

FIGURE 11-7

2. The Groove Music App has buttons to add songs to a playlist. Next time you're listening to a song or album and you think, "I like that song; it should be on a playlist," do one of the following to add the song to a playlist, as shown in **Figure 11-8**:

- **Add a song:** Select a song's Add To button and select a playlist on the pop-up menu that appears.

- **Add all the songs on an album:** Select the Add To button below the album name and select a playlist on the pop-up menu.

Add an album

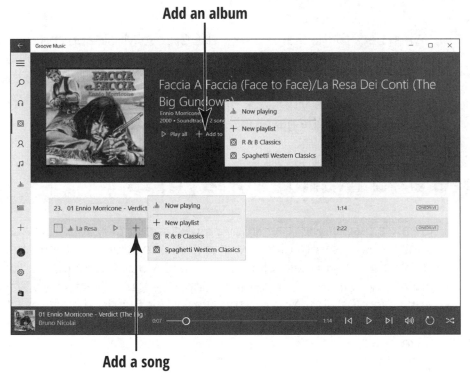

Add a song

FIGURE 11-8

See "Listen to the Music App," earlier in this chapter, if you need help finding and listening to music on your computer.

TIP

3. To play the songs on a playlist, select the name of the playlist on the left side of the screen. The playlist opens, as shown in **Figure 11-9**. Select the Play All button to play the songs in order from first to last.

Of course, you can select any song on the list and select its Play button to play it.

Play all the songs

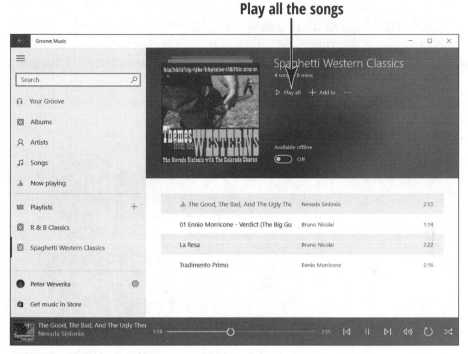

FIGURE 11-9

4. To change the order of songs on a playlist or remove a song, follow these instructions:

- **Change the order of songs:** Drag a song higher or lower on the list with your mouse or finger.

- **Remove a song:** Display the song's context menu and choose Delete from Playlist. To display the context menu, right-click its name with your mouse or hold your finger on the name.

5. Select the Cancel button (refer to **Figure 11-9**) when you finish rearranging the playlist.

TIP

To delete a playlist, open it. Then select the More button and select Delete on the pop-up menu.

Watch Videos

1. Select the Movies & TV app on the Start screen. Microsoft designed this app for watching movies purchased at the Microsoft Store and for watching home-made videos. To watch videos, select the Videos button on the menu bar. The Video screen appears, as shown in **Figure 11-10.** Use the Video screen to watch videos.

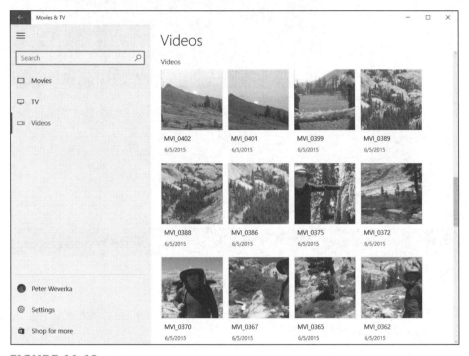

FIGURE 11-10

2. Unless you store your videos in the C:\Users*Your Name*\Videos folder, you don't see any videos. You see the message "Tell us where to look for videos." To tell the Video app where you store your videos, either select the *Tell Us Where to Look for Videos* link or select the Settings button (you'll find it in the lower-left corner of the screen) and select the *Choose Where We Look for Videos* link on the Settings screen. You come to the Build Your Collection screen. Select the Add button, and in the Select Folder dialog box, select the folder where videos are stored and then select the Add This Folder to Videos button. Repeat these instructions to add all the folders where you store videos.

3. To play a video, select it on the Home screen. It appears in the video player screen, as shown in **Figure 11-11**. Along the bottom of this screen are controls for pausing, playing, and changing the volume level. Drag the slider below the video screen to rewind and fast-forward.

Back button

Video controls

Drag to rewind and fast-forward

FIGURE 11-11

4. Select the Back button (refer to **Figure 11-11**) to return to the Movies & TV home screen.

Burn a CD

1. *Burning a CD* means to copy songs from a computer to a CD. Burn a CD so that you can play the songs on your car's CD player or pass along your favorite songs to a friend. To burn a CD, start by opening Windows Media Player, as shown in **Figure 11-12**.

Browse by artist, album, or genre   Drag songs to the list

Search for songs   Save the list   Name the list

FIGURE 11-12

TIP

Earlier in this chapter, "Play and Copy Music for a CD" explains Windows Media Player in detail.

2. Create a playlist so that Windows Media Player knows which songs to burn to the CD. To create a playlist, drag song titles from the music collection on your computer to Unsaved List on the right side of the

screen (refer to **Figure 11-12**). Use these techniques to locate songs and enter them in the playlist:

- **Browse for songs:** Select Artist, Album, or Genre on the left side of the screen. A list of artists, albums, or genres appears. Scroll the list and make a selection so that the song titles appear in the Title column. Then drag a song into Unsaved List.

- **Search for songs:** Enter a search term in the Search box. Then make a selection so that the song titles appear in the Title column and drag songs into Unsaved List.

3. After you assemble the songs, drag their names up or down in the list to put the songs in the order you want.

4. Select the Save List button, type a name for the list (refer to **Figure 11-12**), and press Enter. The names of playlists you create appear under Playlists on the left side of the screen. To listen to a playlist, select its name and click or tap the Play button at the bottom of the screen.

TIP

You can edit a playlist. While the list is playing, drag to change the order of songs, place more songs on the list (follow Step 2), or remove songs from the list by right-clicking and choosing Remove from List.

5. After you create a playlist, you can burn it to a CD. With Windows Media Player open, insert a blank CD in your computer's CD or DVD drive. Then select the Burn tab, as shown in **Figure 11-13**, and drag a playlist from the left side of the screen to Burn List on the right.

6. Note on the right side of the screen whether there is enough disk space to burn all the songs on the list, and if there is enough space, select the Start Burn button. It can take a few minutes to burn a CD. When the job is complete, your computer ejects the CD. I suggest playing it to see whether the songs copied correctly to the CD. While you're at it, label the CD by writing on it with a felt-tip pen. Label the top of the CD, not the bottom.

Drag a playlist

Start the burn

Select the Burn tab

FIGURE 11-13

4

Beyond the Basics

IN THIS PART . . .

Fine-tune Windows 10.

Manage printers and other peripherals.

Manipulate files and folders.

Keep backup copies of files and folders.

Chapter 12
Maintaining Windows 10

Windows 10 is a bit like a car. To make it run well, you have to maintain it.

Windows 10 uses the Security and Maintenance screen to keep you informed of issues that pertain to your computer's health. The screen divides issues into Security and Maintenance sections. The Reliability Monitor can help you pinpoint problems with hardware and software.

Machines such as toaster ovens aren't getting any smarter. Your computer, however, can be programmed to do something it's never done before. To make your computer capable of doing new things, you install new programs. On the other hand, your computer may have some programs that you'll never use and wouldn't miss. You don't have to get rid of them, but doing so is easy enough and frees a little space on your computer.

In this chapter, you work with the Security and Maintenance screen to check your computer's health status. You also install a program on the desktop and, optionally, uninstall one. This chapter also shows how to make your computer work faster by controlling the startup apps, defragmenting your hard disk, and deleting unnecessary system files. You discover how Windows Defender can protect your computer against spyware, viruses, and other foreign invaders. Finally, you see how the Action Center can help you make the best use of your computer.

Explore System Information

1. On the desktop, type **system** in the Search box. This box is located on the left side of the taskbar. The Search panel appears.

2. Select System-Control Panel in the Search panel. The System window shown in **Figure 12-1** appears. This screen is chock-full of information and functions. Note each of the following areas onscreen:

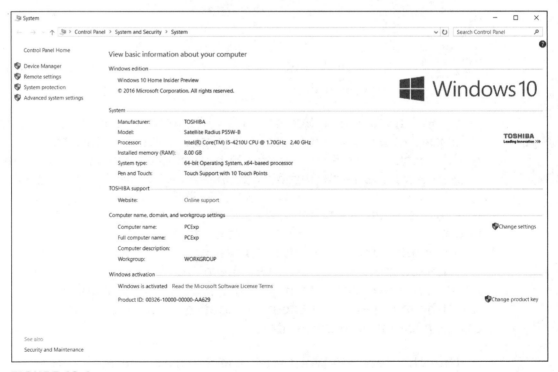

FIGURE 12-1

- **Windows edition:** Of course, you have Windows 10. However, Windows 10 comes in two primary editions: the Home edition, which you are likely to have, and the Pro edition, for computer professionals. You may find information here about so-called Service Packs, which are large collections of updates to Windows 10.

- **System:** This section displays details about your hardware, including the processor, the amount of installed memory (RAM), and other details.

- **Computer name, domain, and workgroup settings:** This information pertains to your network, if you have one. If a computer can't connect to a network, the problem is often related to the name of the Workgroup (a network). The Change Settings function lets you change the Workgroup name to match other computers on the same network. See Chapter 14 for information on networks, including workgroups and homegroups.

- **Windows activation:** In an effort to control software piracy involving bootlegged copies of Windows 10, each copy of Windows 10 must be activated. Odds are that you activated your copy the first time you started your computer. If you don't see *Windows is activated* in this section, select the adjacent link.

TIP

Don't be alarmed by the System information and options. If all goes well, you don't have to use most of what you find here. Some familiarity with this screen will be useful, however, if all doesn't go well later.

Check Your Security and Maintenance Status

1. In the System window (refer to **Figure 12-1**), select Security and Maintenance in the lower-left corner. The Security and Maintenance window appears, as shown in **Figure 12-2**.

Select these headings　　　　　　**Note any messages**

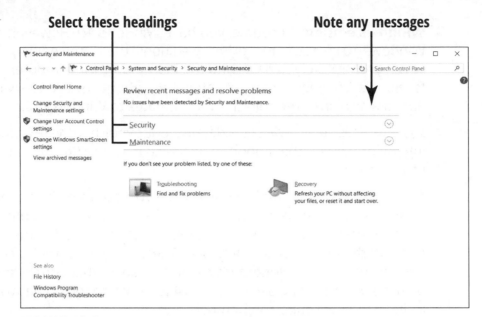

FIGURE 12-2

TIP

Another way to open the Security and Maintenance window is to type **Security and Maintenance** in the Search box on the Windows taskbar.

2. Note any message displayed under Review Recent Messages and Resolve Problems. Ideally, you see *No issues have been detected by Security and Maintenance*. If you see a message concerning a specific problem, select that message for more information.

3. Select the Security heading in the Security and Maintenance window. That section expands to detail security functions. Every option should display *On* or *OK*. Here's a brief description of each item under Security:

- **Network Firewall:** The firewall scans Internet traffic and blocks activity from programs that don't have explicit permission to use Internet access. When you install a program that uses the Internet, you may be asked to approve the connection the first time. The safest practice is to reject online connections that you don't initiate or recognize.

- **Virus Protection:** Having virus protection for your computer is essential. Windows Defender provides antivirus protection, although you can install some other antivirus program.

- **Internet Security Settings:** These settings pertain to your browser. The default settings may be adequate. To learn more, see the following tip.

TIP

I recommend *Using the Internet Safely For Seniors For Dummies* by Nancy Muir and Linda Criddle (John Wiley & Sons, Inc.) as a guide for helping you deal with online security confidently.

- **User Account Control (UAC):** This function notifies you of programs that try to make changes to your system and requires that you confirm any such changes. In particular, UAC lets you know when a program tries to run or install software that may be malicious. When in doubt, say No or Cancel to UAC messages.

- **Windows SmartScreen:** This function blocks you from downloading programs, except through the Microsoft Store, as well as files capable of changing your system maliciously.

- **Microsoft Account:** This one tells you whether your Microsoft Account is set up properly.

4. Select the Maintenance heading to see what that section includes. Functions under Maintenance consist of the following:

- **Check for solutions to problem reports:** This setting is on, allowing Windows 10 to regularly check for solutions to problems it uncovers. (In Step 5, you will run the Reliability History report from this part of the screen.)

- **Automatic Maintenance:** Your computer automatically performs critical updates, security scans, and diagnostics each day.

TIP

If your computer is in a guest room or bedroom, you may want to change the Automatic Maintenance setting to run maintenance tasks at some time other than the default 3:00 a.m. Your computer may actually wake up at that hour for maintenance (although, if your computer is connected to a power strip, you can turn off the power strip and prevent your computer from turning on automatically in the middle of the night). If the computer can't run maintenance at the appointed hour, it will do so at the next opportunity.

- **HomeGroup:** A *homegroup* is a network that allows you to share files and printers between two or more computers. See Chapter 14 for information on networks, including homegroups.

- **File History:** See Chapter 15 for information on using the File History option, which is off by default.

- **Drive status:** *Drives* are hard disks inside or attached to your computer. Your documents, photos, and Windows 10 itself are stored on one or more drives. Ideally, the drive status is *All drives are working properly*. See Chapter 15 for information on backing up and restoring files.

- **Device software:** If a device on your computer needs a driver or other type of software to run properly, you are alerted here. Select Install Device Software to install the software.

The Security and Maintenance window is a troubleshooting tool, so you should check it if you have problems running Windows 10.

5. Under Check for Solutions to Problem Reports, select View Reliability History. As shown in **Figure 12-3**, the Reliability Monitor screen graphs your computer's stability and indicates hardware and software problems, including those you may not be aware of. On this screen, red circles indicate critical events such as computer crashes; blue circles are information about software installation and updates; and yellow triangles indicate warnings about noncritical events (something that didn't crash the computer). Select a day in the graph to display details in the lower portion of the screen.

Reviewing the Reliability Monitor screen helps you distinguish between a one-time glitch and a recurring or worsening problem.

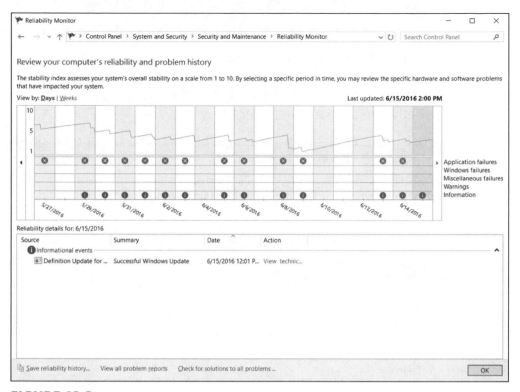

FIGURE 12-3

Install a New Program on the Desktop

1. You can install software that you download from the web or from a CD or DVD for use on the desktop. (Windows 10 apps must be installed through the Microsoft Store.) In this set of steps, you install Windows Photo Gallery, my favorite free program for editing photos. To install Photo Gallery, open your browser and enter **get.live.com** in the address bar. You land on the web page for downloading Windows Essentials (if your browser doesn't take you to this page, go to support.microsoft.com and search for Windows Essentials there). (See Chapter 6 for information on using the Edge browser.)

TIP

If a website offers to install a program automatically, look at that suggestion with suspicion. It may be legitimate or it may be malevolent. Decline downloads from sources that you don't know and trust already.

2. Select the Other Download Options link under the Get It Now button.

3. On the Windows Essentials Download Options web page, scroll to and select the English (United States) link (or select the link that describes your favorite language). In the dialog box that asks you whether to save the file, select Save.

4. Your browser displays a message at the bottom of the browser window, as shown in **Figure 12-4.** Select the Run button. If the User Account Control dialog box appears, select the Yes button to indicate that you want to download and install the program.

Select Run

FIGURE 12-4

5. The Windows Essentials screen appears, as shown in **Figure 12-5, top**. Select Choose the Programs You Want to Install. On the Select Programs to Install screen, deselect everything except Photo Gallery and Movie Maker (one option), as shown in **Figure 12-5, bottom**. Then select Install.

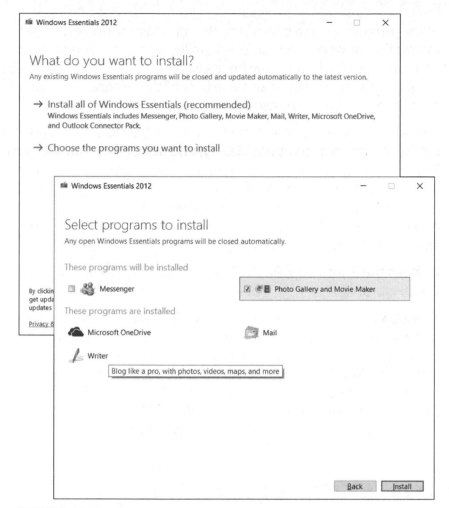

FIGURE 12-5

TIP

Generally, if the installer for a program offers Express or Custom installation options, choose the Express option to let the installer set up the program without further input from you. The Custom or Advanced Settings option allows you to specify where to install the program and, perhaps, which parts of the program to install.

6. A moving bar indicates the progress of the installation, which should take a few minutes. On the screen that indicates installation is done, select the Close button.

TIP

Many programs try to connect to the Internet for updates during installation or when you run the installed program. The first time you run a program, you may be asked whether you want to register the program or configure some aspect of the program. Go with the default (assumed) responses, if you're not sure.

7. To run Photo Gallery, select the Start button, scroll in the alphabetical list of programs to Photo Gallery, and select the Photo Gallery tile. The Service Agreement screen appears. Select the Accept button. Photo Gallery opens on the desktop. If you see the Sign In with Your Email Address screen, enter your Microsoft Account email address and password, select Remember My ID and Password, and then select Sign In. (Or select Cancel.)

8. As does the Photo app, Photo Gallery displays photos from your Photo Library.

TIP

To install a program that comes on a CD or DVD, insert the program disc into your computer's disc drive or tray, label side up (or, if your computer has a vertical disc slot, insert the disc with the label side facing left). The AutoPlay dialog box appears. Select the option to run Install or Setup. User Account Control may ask whether you really want to run this program. (Windows 10 tries to keep you from installing software unintentionally by asking for confirmation.)

Remove Desktop Programs

1. Unlike Windows 10 apps from the Microsoft Store, desktop programs are installed and uninstalled directly through the desktop itself. To see which desktop programs are installed, open the Control Panel. Type **control panel** in the Search box (it's located on the left side of the taskbar) and select Control Panel in the Search panel.

TIP

Most of the functions covered in this chapter are part of Control Panel, which presents many functions for tweaking your computer setup. A fast way to access Control Panel is to right-click the Start button and choose Control Panel on the pop-up menu.

2. In the Control Panel window (shown in **Figure 12-6**), under Programs, select Uninstall a Program. (You don't have to uninstall anything;

you can simply see what the option offers.) You see the Programs window. Select the Uninstall a Program link to open the Programs and Features window.

Uninstall a program or just look

FIGURE 12-6

3. The Programs and Features window lists desktop programs, not Windows 10 apps. Initially, these programs are sorted by name. You may want to see the date you last used each program because a program you haven't used in ages may be a safe one to remove. (Otherwise, skip to Step 5.) Use one of the following techniques to display the date last used:

- **Mouse:** Move the mouse pointer over any column heading, such as Name. Click the right mouse button.

- **Touchscreen:** Tap and hold down on any column heading, such as Name. When a box appears around your fingertip, lift your finger.

4. On the context menu that appears, select More. In the Choose Details window (shown in **Figure 12-7**), select Last Used On and then select the OK button. The Last Used On column appears to the right of all the other columns.

Select the Last Used On option

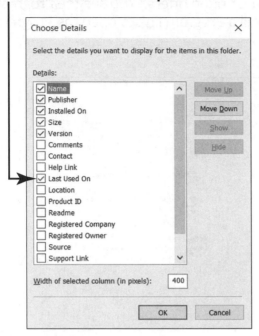

FIGURE 12-7

5. To change a program, select it. For this example, select Windows Essentials, as shown in **Figure 12-8**. You don't have to uninstall Photo Gallery, but if you do, you can follow the steps in the preceding section to reinstall it.

6. Select the Uninstall/Change button (it's located above the list of program names). The Windows Essentials screen offers options to Remove One or More or to Repair All. Some programs offer the Change option to change the program as well. Repair or Change may be useful for a desktop program that you want to keep but isn't running as expected. Select Remove One or More Windows Essential Programs or Cancel. If you select Remove, select Photo Gallery and Movie Maker on the next screen and then select Uninstall. (Your photos are not removed.)

7. If you uninstalled Photo Gallery or another program, it will no longer appear in the Programs and Features window or on the Start screen.

Select to uninstall

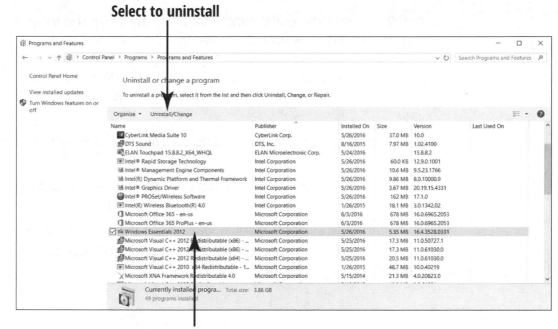

Select a program

FIGURE 12-8

TIP

Just because you can uninstall a program doesn't mean you should. You can simply ignore programs you don't use. Look at a program's name, publisher, and date installed to determine whether you actually use a program. You may recognize a program you installed recently, as opposed to one installed before you got your computer. If you find that it's more productive to remove large programs than small ones, repeat Steps 3 and 4 to group by size.

TIP

Before you uninstall a program that you may want to reinstall later, make sure that you have a copy of it on a CD or DVD (or that you know where to download it from the Web again). You have no undo option when you uninstall a program.

Control Startup Apps

1. Startup apps are applications that start running when you turn on your computer. You might be surprised by how many startup apps run in the background without your knowing it. Occasionally you install new software or download a program from the Internet and discover that it runs automatically whether you like it or not. Sometimes the number of startup apps slows the computer down. To see which apps start running automatically when you turn on your computer, start the Task Manager with one of these techniques:

- **Keyboard:** Press Ctrl+Alt+Del and select Task Manager on the blue screen.

- **Desktop:** On the Desktop, enter **task** in the Search box and then select the Task Manager tile on the menu that appears.

2. Select More Details in the Task Manager window and then select the Startup tab, as shown in **Figure 12-9**. This is the list of applications that start when your computer starts.

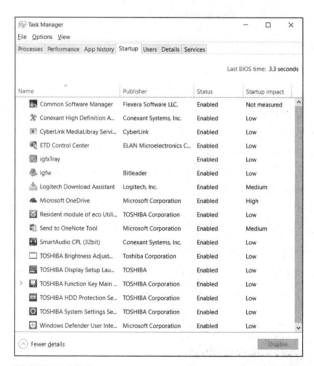

FIGURE 12-9

3. Use one of these techniques to open your browser, go on the Internet, and find out what one of these startup applications does:

- **Mouse:** Right-click an application and choose Search Online.

- **Touchscreen:** Tap and hold down the name of an application. When a box appears around your fingertip, select Search Online.

4. Notice the Startup Impact column in the Task Manager. Applications with a high impact such as Microsoft OneDrive may be slowing down your computer. If you decide that one of these applications is unwanted or is slowing you down, disable it. (Don't worry, you can enable it later on very easily, as I explain shortly.) Disable a startup application with one of these techniques:

- **Mouse:** Right-click the application and choose Disable.

- **Touchscreen:** Tap and hold down the name of the application and choose Disable.

TIP

To enable a startup application in the Task Manager (refer to **Figure 12-9**), display its shortcut menu and choose Enable. The Status column in the Task Manager tells you whether a startup application has been disabled.

Speed Up Your Computer

1. Computers are like people — they tend to slow down with age. However, Windows 10 offers a couple of administrative tools that can make your computer work faster. To find out what these tools are, go to the desktop and type **administrative tools** in the Search box. Then select the Administrative Tools tile to open the Administrative Tools area of the Control Panel, as shown in **Figure 12-10**.

2. Select Defragment and Optimize Drives. The Optimize Drives screen opens, as shown in **Figure 12-11**. When you save a file, the new data you recently added gets placed on the hard disk wherever Windows 10 can find room for it. Consequently, a file is stored in many different places. If you've used your computer for a long time, files become fragmented — the bits and pieces are spread all over the disk and your computer has to work hard to assemble all the pieces to open a file.

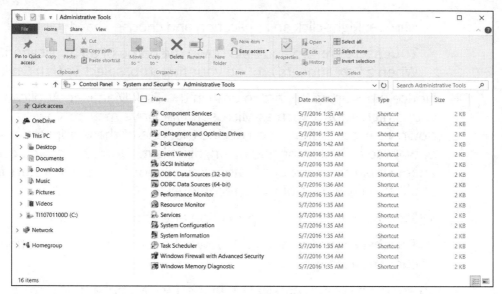

FIGURE 12-10

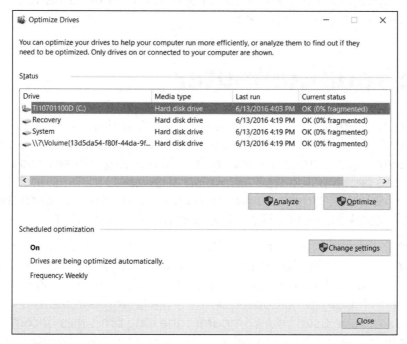

FIGURE 12-11

3. Select the C drive and then select the Optimize button. Windows 10 optimizes your hard disk by moving the bits and pieces of files so that they are stored next to each other on the hard disk. It can take a few minutes or a few hours to optimize a hard disk, but no matter, because Windows 10 conducts this activity in the background and you can go on to do other tasks.

4. Return to the Administrative Tools screen (refer to **Figure 12-10**) and select Disk Cleanup. The Disk Cleanup dialog box appears, as shown in **Figure 12-12**. It tells you how much disk space you can make available on your hard disk by removing unnecessary files.

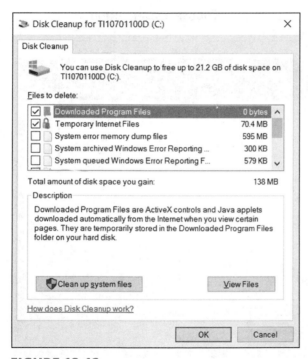

FIGURE 12-12

5. Select the types of files you want deleted, and then select the Clean Up System Files button. A message box appears as the files are deleted from your computer.

Protect Your Computer with Windows Defender

1. In the Search box on the left side of the taskbar, type **windows defender** and then select the Windows Defender tile in the Search panel. The Windows Defender app opens to the Home tab, as shown in **Figure 12-13**. Windows Defender identifies and removes viruses, spyware, and other malefactors from your computer.

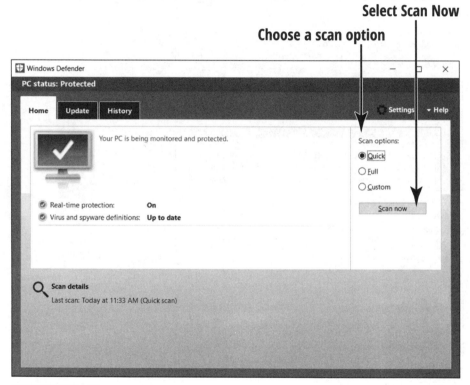

Select Scan Now

Choose a scan option

FIGURE 12-13

2. The Home tab tells you whether virus and spyware definitions are up to date. If they aren't up to date, go to the Update tab and select the Update Definitions button.

TIP

If for some reason you want to turn off Windows Defender (and I can't imagine why anyone would do that), select the Settings button. Doing so opens the Settings app to its Windows Defender screen.

From here, you can turn off the Real-Time Protection setting, which disables Windows Defender.

3. Windows Defender performs "quick scans" in the background each time you run your computer. From time to time, to make sure your computer is thoroughly clean of viruses and spyware, run a full scan. Choose the Full option on the Home tab and then select the Scan Now button (refer to **Figure 12-13**).

4. A full scan can take a long time as Windows Defender examines all the files on your computer for viruses and spyware. You can do other tasks on your computer while the full scan is running. If Windows Defender finds a bad actor, the file with the virus or spyware is quarantined so that it won't harm your computer. When the full scan is complete, a screen like the one in **Figure 12-14** appears. It tells you how many files were examined and whether "threats were detected."

5. If "threats were detected," go to the History tab, select the Quarantined Items option, and select the View Details button to see what the threats were. Then select the Remove All button to remove infected files from your computer.

6. Close Windows Defender.

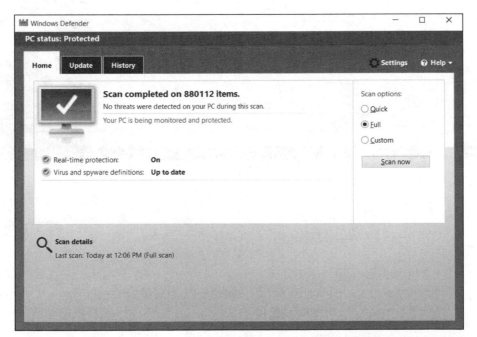

FIGURE 12-14

Use and Manage the Action Center

1. Click or tap the Notifications button in the lower-right corner of the screen, as shown in **Figure 12-15, right**. The Action Center opens (see **Figure 12-15, right**). The purpose of the Action Center is to tell you what's what and help you get things done faster. The top of the Action Center shows notifications from different apps — email messages, weather updates, and the like. Later, in Step 6, I'll show you how to choose which apps deliver these notifications. The bottom of the Action Center provides quick action buttons that you can select to perform different tasks.

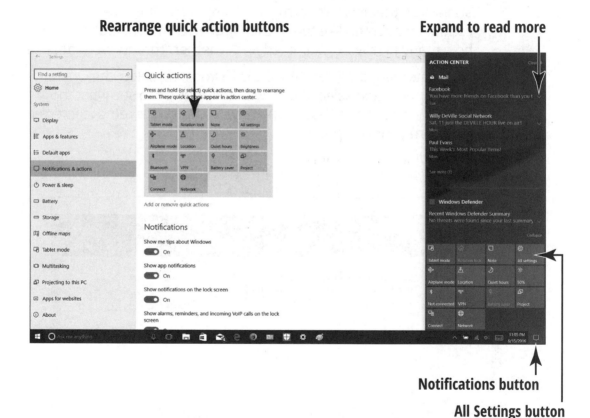

Rearrange quick action buttons

Expand to read more

Notifications button

All Settings button

FIGURE 12-15

TIP

You can also open the Action center by swiping from the left side of the screen or pressing ⊞ +A.

2. Select the Expand button next to a notification at the top of the Action Center (refer to **Figure 12-15, right**). Selecting this button enlarges the notification so you can read it better.

3. Select the All Settings button (refer to **Figure 12-15, right**). The Notification & Actions screen opens, as shown in **Figure 12-15, left**. Use this screen to tell Windows 10 what you want to see in the Action Center.

4. In the Notification & Actions screen, drag the quick actions buttons to rearrange them in the Action Center. As the screen explains, you can rearrange these buttons by dragging them with the mouse or with your finger.

5. Under Notifications in the Notification & Actions screen, turn options on or off to tell Windows whether you want notifications to appear on your screen. Notifications are the sometimes annoying little message boxes that appear when you least expect it in the lower-right corner of the screen.

6. Scroll down the Notification & Actions screen to the area called Show Notifications from These Apps. You see an alphabetical list of apps that can deliver notifications in the top half of the Action Center (refer to in **Figure 12-15, right**). Drag the On/Off sliders to tell Windows 10 which applications you want to deliver notifications.

7. Select the Close button (the X) to close the Settings window.

Chapter 13

Connecting a Printer and Other Devices

E very computer has a screen. Most computers, other than tablets, also have a keyboard and a mouse or other pointing device. You can add a mouse to a laptop that lacks one or replace the keyboard or mouse that came with your computer. Add a printer or a scanner to extend your computer's functionality.

For any hardware add-ons — which tech folk call *peripherals* — Windows 10 has a trick up its sleeve. Thanks to *plug and play* technology, which automatically identifies add-on devices, connecting new devices to your computer can be quite easy.

In this chapter, you explore the devices connected to your computer, as well as options available for those devices. You find out how to access devices connected to your computer and also calibrate a touchscreen to make it work better for you.

Trust USB Plug and Play for Hardware

You may find many kinds of add-on devices useful:

» A **printer** lets you, well, print documents and photos. Your choices for printers include black and white versus color, and inkjet versus laser printer. A multifunction printer also works as a copier, scanner, and fax machine.

» A **digital camera** captures photos that you can copy to your computer to enjoy and to share with others. See Chapter 10 for information on working with photos.

» A **scanner** enables you to make digital images of old photos or documents so that you can view them onscreen.

» An **external hard drive** stores backup copies of your files. See Chapter 15 for information on adding a hard drive to your computer.

» An additional or replacement **pointing device** (your mouse is a pointing device), including a trackball or a pen with a tablet, may be more comfortable to use than what came with your computer. Switching between pointing devices helps you avoid repetitive stress. A wireless mouse eliminates the hassle of dealing with a cord. Some people like to add a mouse as an alternative to their laptop's built-in touchpad.

» A **microphone** is crucial for communicating by voice with your computer, through speech recognition, or with your friends over the Internet. A combination headset with microphone may produce the clearest sound.

» A **video camera** (or *webcam*) is essential for video phone calls *à la* the Jetsons. See Chapter 10 for information on using a webcam.

The majority of these devices connect using *USB* (Universal Serial Bus) technology. When you connect a device to your computer using a USB cable to the USB port (see **Figure 13-1**), the device identifies itself to the computer. This identification process is called *plug and play*. Ideally, you connect your device, and it simply works.

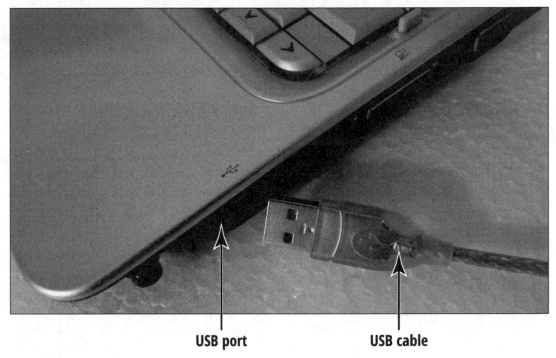

USB port   USB cable

FIGURE 13-1

Windows 10 uses a *device driver* to communicate with an add-on device. The driver is really a program that tells Windows 10 how to run the device. When you connect a device, such as a printer, Windows 10 looks for a driver (in this case, a *printer driver*). That driver may be built into Windows 10, come on a disc that's packaged with the device, or need to be downloaded from the Internet, either automatically by Windows 10 or manually by you.

Every computer has at least a couple of USB ports. Some are in the front, and others are in the back of the computer and harder to reach. If your computer doesn't have enough ports, you can add more by buying a USB hub, which is a small box with two to four USB ports. If a port is hard to reach with a device's cable, you can buy a USB extension cable. Office supply stores may have hubs and cables.

Bluetooth is a wireless technology for adding devices to your computer. If your computer has Bluetooth, you can use Bluetooth as well as USB to add some devices, especially a microphone or headset.

See All Devices

1. Choose Settings on the Start menu. The Settings window opens. Choose Devices to open the Printers & Scanners category of the Devices window, as shown in **Figure 13-2, top**. Note the printers and scanners (if any) that are connected to your computer.

FIGURE 13-2

2. Select the Connected Devices category in the Devices window, as shown in **Figure 13-2, bottom,** and scroll down the screen to see all your devices. Devices listed may include your monitor, speakers, headphones, keyboard, mouse, and more. Devices shared through your homegroup or network also appear here. For information on adjusting device settings, see the "Access Device Options on the Desktop" section, later in the chapter.

Some, but not all, devices display information below the device name. A network device may display *Offline* (not accessible) or it may display nothing if it is accessible. A printer may display *Ready* or it may display nothing if the printer isn't ready.

You are unlikely to need the Add a Device button because most devices are added *automagically* (that's a word nerds like to use). However, if you select Add a Device, Windows 10 scans for additional hardware. No harm in doing so.

Connect a Printer or Other Device

1. Take your printer out of the box. Keep all the packing material together until you know you won't need to return the printer. Arrange all the components for easy access. In addition to the printer, you'll probably find ink cartridges or a toner cartridge, a power cable, and a CD with printer software. Read the setup instructions that come with your printer.

Some of these steps apply to other devices, such as a mouse, a webcam, or a microphone. Printers often have more packaging and require more assembly than other devices.

2. Remove all tape from the printer. Most printers ship with the print mechanism locked in place to prevent it from moving during shipping. Look for brightly colored tape, paper, or plastic indicating what you need to move or remove to release the print mechanism.

3. Put the printer within cable length of your computer. Insert the ink or toner cartridge before you turn on the printer for the first time. Place some paper in the paper drawer or tray. Connect the printer to the power supply. Plug the printer cable into the printer and into the computer.

Your printer may have come with a disc with a printer driver and other software. You don't need that disc unless Windows 10 fails to correctly install a driver automatically.

4. Turn on the printer. You may see some informational messages as Windows 10 handles the configuration.

5. To confirm that your printer is installed properly, see the preceding section, "See All Devices."

Access Device Options on the Desktop

1. For more control over device setup, enter **devices and printers** in the Search box on the taskbar. Then select Devices and Printers to display the window shown in **Figure 13-3**.

TIP

You can open the Devices and Printers window (see **Figure 13-3**) from the Connected Devices category of the Devices window (refer to **Figure 13-2, bottom**). To do so, scroll to the bottom of the Connected Devices category and select Devices and Printers.

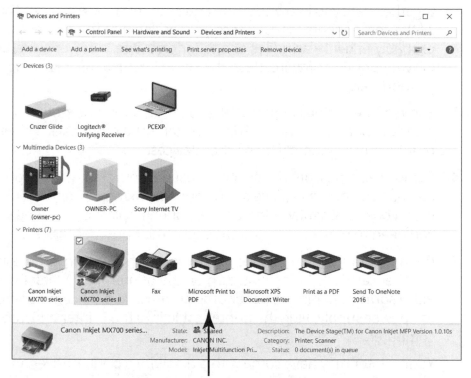

Select a device to access options

FIGURE 13-3

2. The Device and Printers window shows the devices attached to your computer, including the computer itself, the display (or monitor), external add-on devices (such as a hard drive, flash drive, or memory card), and the mouse.

TIP

Most of these devices also appear in the Connected Devices category of the Devices app. However, you'll find options under Devices and Printer that aren't available in the Devices app, such as settings for devices.

TIP

Windows 10 automatically installs the Microsoft XPS Document Writer. This device doesn't print but does create files that you can print later using a real printer. For example, if you're in a coffee shop and want to print a web page or an email message, you can use this device and then open the file it creates when your computer is connected to a printer. (That file will open in Reader.)

3. Double-click or double-tap the device you want to examine. This action opens the device's properties in a window with options or in a smaller box with limited information and options. (Older devices have more limited information.) **Figure 13-4** shows information about a printer. When you're finished reviewing the information or selecting available options, return to the previous screen using one of these methods:

- If a small box is open, close it.

- If a full-screen dialog box is open, select the back arrow or select Devices and Printers near the top of the window.

FIGURE 13-4

4. Display the context menu of options for your printer (or any device) using one of these methods: Click the right mouse button, or tap and hold until you see a small box appear under your finger and then release. Select Printer Properties from the context menu. (Oddly, the menu also has a separate Properties option — be sure to select Printer Properties instead.)

5. In the Properties window, select the Print Test Page button. Another window opens indicating *A test page has been sent to your printer*. Select Close.

If a test page doesn't print, check that both ends of the cable are plugged in properly and make sure the printer is turned on. Try to print a test page again. For more help, contact the printer manufacturer or the store where you bought the printer, or search the web.

If you're having problems with any device, select the Troubleshoot option on the context menu to open a guided troubleshooting program that will walk you through options for resolving problems with the device.

The top of the Devices and Printers window has the Add a Device and Add a Printer button, but you need to use them only if Windows 10 doesn't automatically detect and install your device. With USB and plug and play, most devices install automatically.

Calibrate Your Touchscreen

1. If you have a problem accurately selecting objects on your screen using touch, you can calibrate your screen alignment. In this case, calibrating means to help Windows 10 understand what constitutes a tap on the screen. On the Start screen, type **tablet pc**. Then select the Tablet PC tile in the Search results panel.

2. In the Tablet PC Settings window, select the Calibrate button, as shown in **Figure 13-5**. User Account Control may ask you to confirm that you want to run the Digitizer Calibration Tool. If so, select Yes.

If your touchscreen is badly calibrated, you may not be able to tap the Calibrate button. In that case, plug in a mouse to make the selection, and then continue using touch.

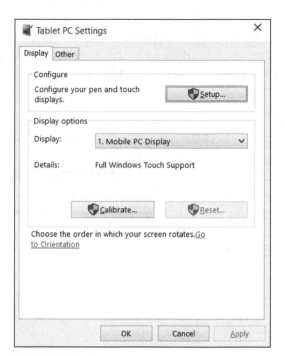

FIGURE 13-5

3. The screen displays lines around its perimeter, forming a box near the edge of the screen and a second box inside the first about half an inch from the edge. Lines connect these boxes near each corner. The result is 16 intersections. Starting at the upper-left corner, use your finger or a stylus to tap each intersection, which displays two short black lines forming crosshairs. As you touch each intersection, Windows 10 measures your touch and adjusts touch settings accordingly. After each touch is recorded, the crosshairs move to the next intersection to the right. (If the crosshairs don't move, tap the previous intersection again.) As the crosshairs move, tap the highlighted intersection, left to right, down, and then left to right again. The process takes much longer to read about than to do.

TIP

If Windows 10 doesn't recognize your touch, it won't continue with the process. The screen says *Right-click anywhere to return to the last calibration point*. What if you don't have a mouse? Tap and hold until you see the little box under your fingertip, and then release — that's the touch equivalent of a click of the right mouse button.

4. After you have selected each of the 16 calibration points in turn, a box pops up asking whether you want to save the calibration data. Select OK unless you think something went wrong. In that case, select Cancel.

TIP

It's unlikely but possible that you can't continue to the end of the process. If so, the screen says *Press the Esc button to close the tool*. What if you don't have a keyboard? In that case, press and hold the Windows button (with the four-part Windows logo) on the tablet edge as you also press the power button, and then release both. On the next screen, select Task Manager. In the Task Manager window, select Digitizer Calibration Tool, and then select the End Task button. (Makes one yearn for an Esc key.)

Chapter 14

Organizing Your Documents

All the data inside your computer is stored on a disk. Your computer has a primary disk, formally called the internal *hard drive*. You may see this disk referred to as the C: drive. (The terms *drive* and *disk* are interchangeable.)

The contents of a disk are organized into individual files. When you save a document, you create a file on a disk. Many other files on the disk belong to the programs you use, including the thousands of files that make up Windows 10.

Disks also are organized into *folders*, which are containers for files. For its own files, Windows 10 has a main folder that contains dozens of other folders (called *subfolders*). Inside or below that user account folder, Windows 10 creates more folders to help you organize your files by type. For example, by default all your photos go into the Pictures folder, and all your documents go into the Documents folder.

In this chapter, you search for files and explore your disk, folders, and documents. You work with File Explorer as you create new folders to organize documents and move files from one folder to another. You also copy files from your hard disk to other disks to take with you or give to other people. File management is much more exciting than it may sound so far. Finally, this chapter explains how to create and join a homegroup so that you can share your files with others over a home network.

Find a Misplaced File

1. To search for a misplaced file, begin in the Search box. This box is located on the left side of the taskbar. Type the name of a document or photo you have on your computer. The search results panel appears, as shown in **Figure 14-1**.

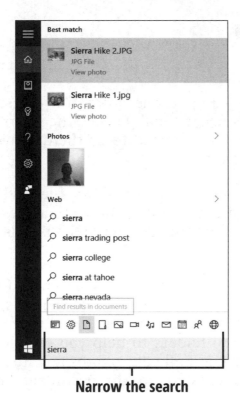

Narrow the search

FIGURE 14-1

2. Initially, the search panel shows all and sundry — settings, apps, files, websites, and other search opportunities — in the search results.

If you don't see the document or photo you want, narrow the list of items by selecting the Find Results in Documents button Find Results in Photos button on the bottom of the search panel (refer to **Figure 14-1**). These options narrow the search to items on your computer.

3. To open a file, select it in the search results and select OK. If more than one application on your computer is capable of opening the file, you may see the How Do You Want to Open This File? dialog box, as shown in **Figure 14-2**. Select an application to open the file.

Choose an application

Select to always open files of this type with the application you choose

FIGURE 14-2

TIP

The How Do You Want to Open This File? dialog box offers a means of telling Windows 10 to always open files of a certain type with a particular application. In **Figure 14-2**, for example, the dialog box lists applications that can open PNG files (PNG is a type of graphics file). In this case, if I wanted to always open PNG files with the Photo Gallery app, I would select the Always Use This App to Open check box and then select Photo Gallery in the dialog box.

4. Close the app that opens the file by using one of these methods:

   • Click or tap the Close button (the *X* located in the upper-right corner of the screen).

   • Press Alt+F4.

TIP

Strictly speaking, if you find what you're looking for, stop looking. (No extra charge for pearls of wisdom.) In this case, however, keep looking because doing so reveals important information about how files are organized and how you can take control of that organization.

5. On the desktop, select the File Explorer icon (the yellow folder) in the taskbar. File Explorer opens. Note the *Ribbon,* which is the collapsible toolbar at the top of the window, as shown in **Figure 14-3**.

TIP

On the Ribbon, tools are grouped by tabs, which in File Explorer consist of File, Home, Share, and View, as well as other tabs that appear based on the selection. Tabs are further divided into sections, labeled below the related tools. (Note, for example, the Clipboard section on the Home tab.) To expand the Ribbon, select the up arrow at the far right of the tabs. Collapse the Ribbon by selecting the down arrow. Select a tab to display its tools, regardless of whether the Ribbon is expanded or collapsed.

6. Select This PC on the left side of the File Explorer window, and then select the box labeled *Search* (probably followed by *This PC*), below the Ribbon and to the right. Type the same search term you used in Step 1. As you type, File Explorer displays any matching files, highlighting the text that matches. **Figure 14-4** shows the results of a search on my computer using the search term *sierra*.

TIP

On a touchscreen, the virtual keyboard doesn't appear on the desktop until you select the keyboard icon on the right side of the taskbar.

Collapse or expand the Ribbon

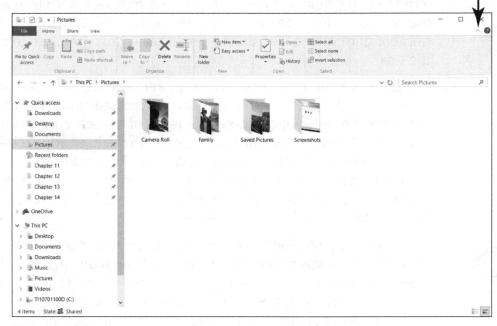

FIGURE 14-3

Type your search term

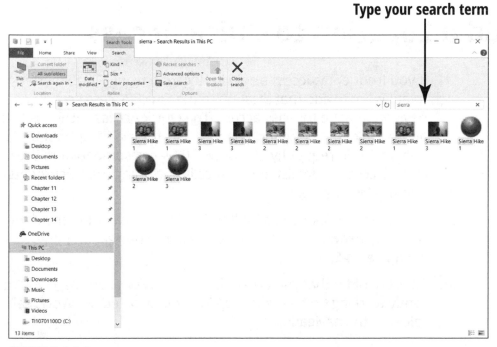

FIGURE 14-4

TIP

If the search results include too many files, making it hard to see the one you want, type more of the filename in the Search box. The number of matching files should decrease as you type more text in the box.

7. The *focus* of a search — where File Explorer searches — determines what files and folders are found. In Step 6, you selected This PC, making all the files on your computer the focus of the search. Accordingly, Windows 10 searched for files and folders throughout your computer. To change the focus of your search to the Pictures folder, select the Pictures folder in the Navigation pane. Then select the box labeled Search and enter your search term again. The search results focus on files in the Pictures folder.

TIP

You can use Search Tools in the Ribbon to refine a search, as needed. Start a search and then select the Search tab. In the section labeled Refine, select Date Modified and then select a time period ranging from Today to Last Year. Select Kind to limit the search to specific types of files. You can even select by size and other properties.

Add a Location to Quick Access

1. If you frequently access a specific location using File Explorer, you might want to add that location to the Quick Access section of the navigation pane for easy access. The Quick Access section is located at the top of the navigation pane. It lists folders in alphabetical order that you visit frequently. Windows 10 places some folders in the Quick Access folder list automatically, including the Documents folder and the Pictures folder.

2. Display the Quick Access folders. To do so, click or tap the right-pointing arrow next to Quick Access in the navigation pane, as shown in **Figure 14-5.**

3. Select a folder that you access frequently. For example, if you're currently working on files you keep in a folder called My Work, select that folder in the navigation pane.

Display Quick Access folders

Select a folder and select Pin to Quick Access

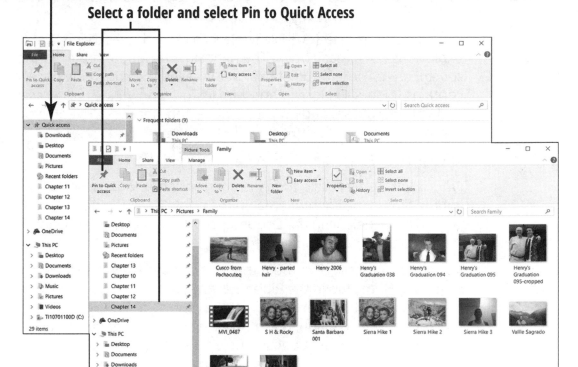

FIGURE 14-5

4. On the Home tab, select the Pin to Quick Access button (refer to **Figure 14-5**). The name of the folder you selected in Step 3 now appears in the Quick Access folder list. Notice the pin beside its name.

5. Select your folder in the Quick Access folder list. Next time you want to get to this folder, you can get there quickly by selecting Quick Access in the navigation pane and then selecting your folder.

TIP

To remove a folder from the Quick Access list, select the folder you want to remove. Then right-click the folder and choose Unpin from Quick Access on the shortcut list.

Use File Explorer for Easy Access to Files

1. On the desktop, select the File Explorer icon in the taskbar if File Explorer is not already open. The right side of Explorer is called the *content area*. The left side of Explorer is called the *navigation pane* and contains folders. Explorer starts with its focus on your Quick Access and This PC folders, and on your C drive and Network drives (if your computer is connected to a network).

The keyboard shortcut to open File Explorer is ⊞+E.

TIP

2. On the left, select Music, then Pictures, and then Videos, while noting the files in the content area on the right. Many Windows 10 apps store files by default in the Documents, Music, Pictures, and Videos folders. Select the Documents folder again.

3. To create a practice document that you can use in later sections, select the Home tab in the Ribbon. In the New section, select New Item and then select Text Document, as shown in **Figure 14-6**. (If you don't see this option, make sure that the Documents folder is selected.) An empty text document is created and the words *New Text Document* are highlighted so that you can type a new name. Type **practice file**. (You'll rename this file in a later section.) Feel free to repeat this step to create additional items for practice, such as Microsoft Word Documents or Bitmap Images.

On a touchscreen, the virtual keyboard doesn't appear on the desktop until you select the keyboard icon on the right side of the taskbar.

TIP

4. Select the View tab in the Ribbon. In the Layout section, select each option, such as Extra Large Icons and Large, Medium, and Small Icons. If you see a downward-pointing triangle on the right edge of the Layout options, select that triangle to display even more options. Try them all, if you like.

Certain layouts are better for certain purposes. For example, photos are easier to recognize as Extra Large Icons than as a List. **Figure 14-7** shows my documents using the Details view, which includes the date the file was modified.

TIP

The more time you spend in File Explorer, the more worthwhile it is to explore the Ribbon as you need it.

TIP

Select New Item to create an empty document

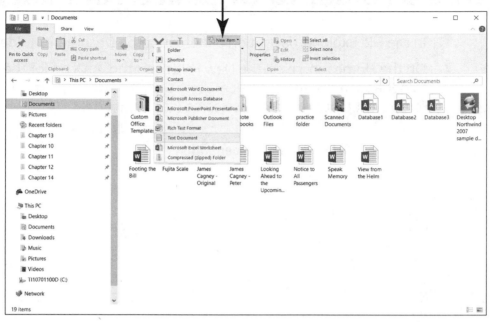

FIGURE 14-6

Details view shows the file modification date

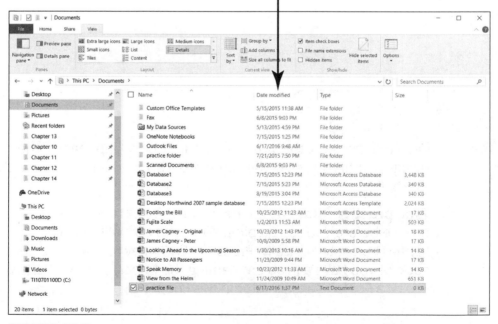

FIGURE 14-7

Create a Folder to Organize Your Files

1. In the File Explorer navigation pane, select the Documents folder.

2. On the Home tab, select the New Folder button. An icon for the new folder appears in the content area on the right, with the name *New folder* next to it and already selected (see **Figure 14-8**).

Select the New Folder button

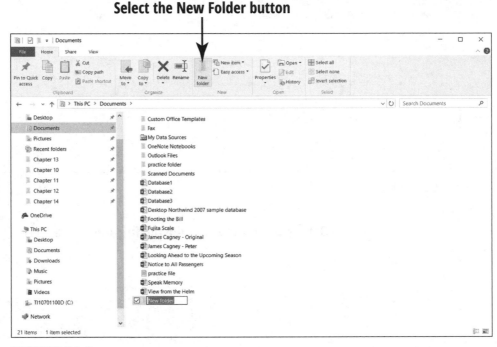

FIGURE 14-8

TIP

On a touchscreen, the virtual keyboard doesn't appear on the desktop until you select the keyboard icon on the right side of the taskbar.

3. Type **practice folder** as the new name. Don't move the cursor or mouse before you start typing. Your new text will replace the high-lighted text automatically. Press the Enter key to make the new name stick. (If you have a problem naming the folder, see the "Rename a File or a Folder" section, later in this chapter.)

4. Open your new folder by double-clicking or double-tapping its icon. Notice that the content area is empty.

5. To return to the Documents folder, select Documents in the navigation pane.

TIP

Don't worry too much about creating folders, because the folders that Windows 10 provides may be all you ever need. As you accumulate more files, however, placing them into other folders can help you stay organized. In the Documents folder, for example, you might create a subfolder called Finances for files related to income, expenses, and investments, and another subfolder called Family for family-related documents. Which folders and subfolders to create and how to name them depends entirely on your own sense of order.

Use Check Boxes to Select Files

1. In File Explorer, you select files to move, copy, rename, or delete. You can add a check box to make selecting multiple files easier. In Explorer, select the View tab and then select the Options button. The Folder Options window appears. Select the View tab (in the Folder Options window, not in the Explorer Ribbon), as shown in **Figure 14-9**. Scroll through the Advanced Settings box until you see Use Check Boxes to Select Items, and then select that check box. Select the OK button.

2. Select the Documents folder (or any folder that contains more than one file). To select a file, click or tap the area to the left of the filename. (You won't see the check box until you select it with a tap or a click, or hover over it with the mouse pointer.) Repeat to select additional files. If you want to deselect a file, select the check box again to remove the check mark. Close the window after you've seen how these check boxes work. **Figure 14-10** shows two selected files.

TIP

If you want to select only a single file, you can select anywhere on the filename. You use the check box when you want to select more than one file at a time.

The Home tab has other methods for selecting. Select All does just what it says — selects all objects in a folder or library. Select None works similarly. Invert Selection switches the selection. For example, if I chose Invert Selection in the context of **Figure 14-10,** the two selected files would be deselected and all the other files would be selected. Sometimes it's easier to select the files you don't want and then invert the selection.

Select this option

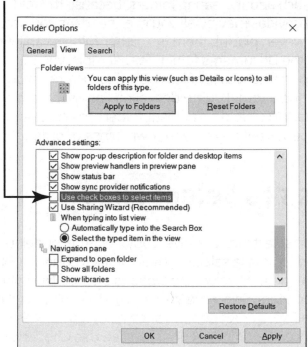

FIGURE 14-9

Select a file by using its check box

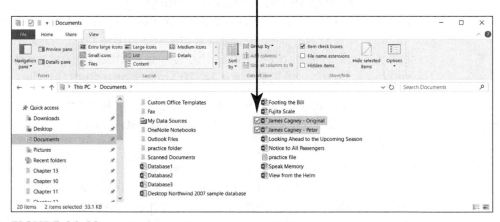

FIGURE 14-10

Add the Undo Button to File Explorer

1. You can add a button to File Explorer to undo an action, such as moving, renaming, or deleting a file. Above the Home tab, select the rather small down-pointing arrow to display the Customize Quick Access Toolbar list, as shown in **Figure 14-11**.

Customize the Quick Access toolbar

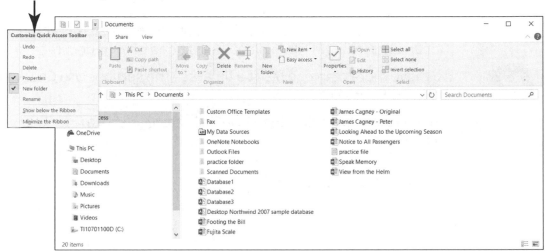

FIGURE 14-11

2. Select the Undo option from the drop-down list. The Undo button, which sports a blue arrow curving to the left, appears immediately to the left of the arrow you clicked in Step 1. You can undo most — but not all — actions in File Explorer by clicking or tapping this button immediately after the action. (Time isn't the issue. You can do something and then undo it a year later if you don't do anything in the meantime.)

TIP

The keyboard shortcut for undo is Ctrl+Z. This shortcut works regardless of whether the Undo button is on the screen.

Sometimes, you can undo a series of actions by repeating the undo function.

3. Select the Customize Quick Access Toolbar button again. Note that you can also add the Redo button, which, as you would expect, undoes the undo. All the other options appear also on larger buttons on the Home tab, so you don't need to add them to the Quick Access toolbar.

Move a File from One Folder to Another

1. You can move files to organize them. For this exercise, select the Documents folder in File Explorer. Select one of your documents.

TIP

To move more than one file at a time, see the section "Use Check Boxes to Select Files."

On the Home tab, select the Move To button, as shown in **Figure 14-12**.

Select the Move To button

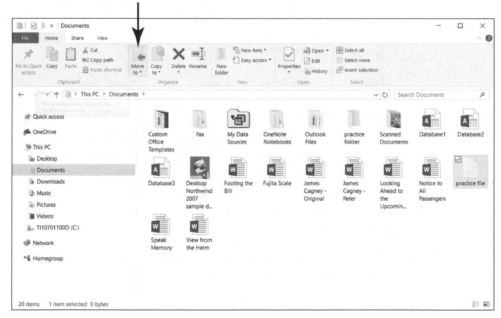

FIGURE 14-12

2. If you see the location you want in the drop-down list, you can select that location. However, for practice, select Choose Location. A window opens, showing every possible location, as shown in **Figure 14-13**. Select Documents and then select the practice folder I tell you how to create in the section "Create a Folder to Organize Your Files," earlier in this chapter. (You can also select the Make New Folder button and name that folder.) Finally, select the Move button.

Select a location

FIGURE 14-13

Unless you move many files or large files, you may not see any indication that the move was completed.

3. In Explorer, select the folder to which you moved your file. There it is!

Note that the Copy To button in File Explorer works similarly, except that the original file stays where it is and a copy is created in the new location.

TIP

Use these same steps to move a subfolder from one folder to another. However, don't move folders that Windows 10 creates.

TIP

You can move a file in a single step. Click and drag or tap and drag the file to the desired folder. When the file is over the folder, release the mouse button or lift your finger. Although this method can make moving easier, it can also make moving a file to the wrong destination easier. Double-check that the file ends up where you want it before going on to other things.

Rename a File or a Folder

1. You can change the name of any file or folder you create. (Don't rename files in the Windows or Program Files folders.) For this exercise, select the Documents folder in File Explorer. Then select one of your files.

TIP

To rename more than one file at a time, see the section "Use Check Boxes to Select Files," earlier in this chapter. On completion of the rename operation, the files you selected will share the name you provide; each file will have a unique number added to the name, starting with *(1)*.

2. On the Home tab, select the Rename button. In the content area, the current name of the file or folder is selected, as shown in **Figure 14-14**. If you type anything while the text is selected, you erase the current name, which is convenient if the new name is completely different from the old name. If you want to keep most of the current name and edit it, select inside the name or press the left- or right-arrow key to move to the place in the name where you want to type new text.

3. Type the new name, which can be more than 200 characters long (although a dozen characters may be more than enough). You can capitalize letters and use spaces and dashes, but you can't use slashes or asterisks, which Windows 10 reserves for other purposes.

TIP

On a touchscreen, the virtual keyboard doesn't appear on the desktop until you select the keyboard icon on the right side of the taskbar.

Rename your file

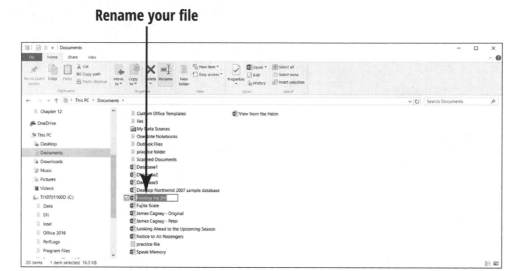

FIGURE 14-14

4. When you've typed the new name, press the Enter key to finish the process.

Delete a File or Folder

1. You can delete any of your files that you no longer need. (Don't delete files in the Windows or Program Files folders.) For this exercise, select the Documents folder in File Explorer. Then select one of your files.

TIP

To delete more than one file at a time, see the section "Use Check Boxes to Select Files," earlier in this chapter.

2. On the Home tab, select the X on the Delete button.

TIP

The keyboard shortcut to delete the selected file is the Delete key (surprise!).

3. A confirmation dialog box appears and asks whether you really want to delete the file, as shown in **Figure 14-15**. Here's your chance to change your mind, if you want. However, for this exercise, select Yes in the dialog box to delete the file.

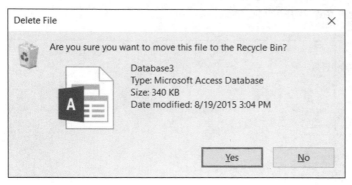

FIGURE 14-15

TIP

If you don't see a confirmation dialog box like the one in **Figure 14-15**, tell Windows 10 that you want to see this dialog box when you delete files and folders. Select the bottom third of the Delete button to display the drop-down list and then select Show Recycle Confirmation.

4. Select another file, and then select the X on the Delete button. The Delete File confirmation window appears. This time, select No to cancel the operation.

TIP

You can permanently delete a file, in which case it will not be sent to the Recycle Bin. Select the file, select the bottom of the Delete button, and then select the Permanently Delete option.

Get Back a File or Folder You Deleted

1. Normally, when you delete a file or folder, Windows 10 moves the object to the Recycle Bin. Objects remain in the Recycle Bin indefinitely, allowing you to restore something you deleted long after you did so. To open the Recycle Bin, go to the desktop and double-click or double-tap the Recycle Bin icon. The Recycle Bin opens, as shown in **Figure 14-16**.

2. If many files or folders are listed in the Recycle Bin window, type the name of the item you want in the Search box in the top-right corner of the window. If any files match what you type, they appear in the content area.

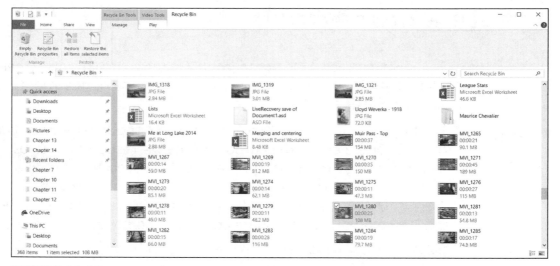

FIGURE 14-16

Note that on a touchscreen, the virtual keyboard doesn't appear on the desktop until you select the keyboard icon on the right side of the taskbar.

3. To restore a file or folder to its original location, select the file or folder in the Recycle Bin window. On the Manage tab, select Restore the Selected Items (refer to **Figure 14-16**). The selected file or folder returns to the folder it was in before it was deleted.

TIP

If Windows 10 needs disk space, it will automatically clear out the oldest files in the Recycle Bin first. If you want to get rid of everything in the Recycle Bin, select the Manage tab and then select Empty Recycle Bin. After you empty the Recycle Bin, you can't undo your action.

TIP

Don't select the Restore All Items button, because doing so puts every single item in the Recycle Bin back in its original location. Most of the files in the Recycle Bin are probably files that you really meant to delete. Choosing this command would be like dumping the trash can on your living-room floor to find a penny you threw away.

See Chapter 15 for information on backing up and restoring files.

Create a Homegroup

1. On the Start screen, type **homegroup**. On the search results screen, select HomeGroup – Control Panel. This opens the HomeGroup screen in the Control Panel.

TIP

A *homegroup* is a simple *network*, which is a connection between two or more computers for the purpose of sharing resources, such as an Internet connection, files, printers, and storage. One user on a network creates a homegroup that other users join, if they choose. Users can share files stored in these folders: Pictures, Videos, Music, and Documents. They can share printers and other devices, as well.

2. Select the Create a Homegroup button and click or tap Next on the following screen.

3. For each folder and device that you want to share, choose Shared or Not Shared on the drop-down menu, as shown in **Figure 14-17**.

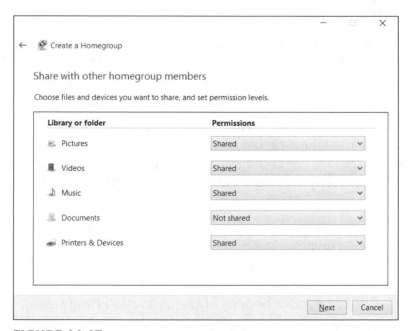

FIGURE 14-17

TIP

Folders and devices shared in the homegroup will appear in File Explorer and other places where you save or open files.

4. Click Next. The Use This Password screen appears, as shown in **Figure 14-18**. The password required by other users to join your homegroup appears in the box. When people want to join your homegroup, they need this password. "Write down this password," the screen suggests.

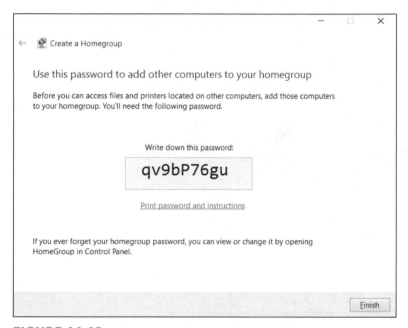

Before you can access files and printers located on other computers, add those computers to your homegroup. You'll need the following password.

Write down this password:

qv9bP76gu

Print password and instructions

If you ever forget your homegroup password, you can view or change it by opening HomeGroup in Control Panel.

FIGURE 14-18

5. Select the Finish button.

6. Open File Explorer. In the navigation pane on the left, select Homegroup and then select your name. You see items such as folders and printers that you share with the homegroup, as shown in **Figure 14-19, top**. If others have joined your homegroup, you see their names as well. You can select a name to see which items other members share with the group.

7. Select Homegroup in the navigation pane, as shown in **Figure 14-19, bottom**. Then select the HomeGroup tab if it isn't already selected. This tab offers buttons for managing your homegroup:

   • **Share Libraries and Devices:** Opens the Sharing screen (refer **Figure 14-17**) so that you can redefine which folders and devices you share with the homegroup.

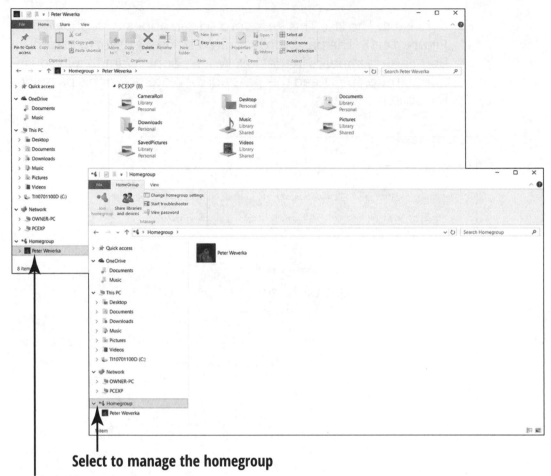

Select to manage the homegroup

Select to see what you share

FIGURE 14-19

- **Change Homegroup Settings:** Opens a Control Panel screen from which you can change the password, leave the homegroup, and choose advanced settings.

- **Start Troubleshooter:** Starts a troubleshooter for fixing problems with the homegroup.

- **View Password:** Shows you the homegroup's password. Go here when someone wants to join the group and needs the password to do so.

TIP

To leave a homegroup, go to the Homegroup tab and select the Change Homegroup settings button. The Change Homegroup Settings screen opens. Select the Leave the Homegroup link. On the Leave the Homegroup screen, select Leave the Homegroup.

Join a Homegroup

1. On the Start screen, type **homegroup**. On the search results screen, select HomeGroup – Control Panel. You come to the HomeGroup screen in the Control Panel. If the owner of another PC in your household has already created a homegroup, the screen tells you as much. It says that another person "has created a homegroup on the network."

TIP

You can also join a homegroup by selecting Homegroup in the navigation pane of File Explorer.

2. Select the Join Now button and select Next on the following screen. You see the Share screen (refer to **Figure 14-17**). On this screen, declare which folders and which devices you want to share with others in the homegroup, and click or tap the Next button.

3. On the following screen, enter the password to the homegroup and then click Next. If all goes well, you are admitted to the homegroup, and you can select the Finish button.

TIP

The person who created the homegroup can give you the password. If that person doesn't remember it, he or she can select the View Password button on the Homegroup tab (refer to **Figure 14-19, bottom**) to see what the password is.

4. Open File Explorer and, under Homegroup in the navigation pane, select the name of the homegroup you joined. The content area shows you the names of folders and devices shared by members of the homegroup. Select a folder or device to access it.

Chapter 15

Backing Up and Restoring Files

Some of your files — photos and documents — are priceless. If you accidentally delete a treasured file, what can you do but cry? You can insure your well-being by creating copies of your documents and photos.

The best insurance involves storing copies of files on devices separate from your computer. Such devices include the following:

» **Flash drive and memory card:** Carry your files when you're away from your computer by storing them on a portable storage device. For example, you can store files on a USB *flash drive* (also called a *thumb drive*), which is about the size of a disposable cigarette lighter, or a *memory card,* which is the size of a postage stamp and is most often used in laptop computers and digital cameras. Common capacities for flash drives and memory cards range from 2 to 64GB.

TIP

A *gigabyte* (GB) of storage can hold thousands of files, but you'll be amazed by how quickly you can fill that space.

» **External hard drive:** This type of drive has a much higher capacity than a flash drive, making it ideal for backing up all your files — the best insurance. Affordable external hard drives range from 500GB to 3 TB.

TIP

A *terabyte* (TB) of storage is equal to a thousand gigabytes, which should be enough room to back up everything on your computer.

» **Network drive:** If your computer connects to a home network, you may be able to copy files to other devices on the network. For example, you can use a large-capacity network drive to back up files from more than one computer.

» **OneDrive:** Your Microsoft Account comes with gigabytes of free storage in the cloud (on the Internet). Anything stored in OneDrive is duplicated on additional computers you log in to with the same Microsoft Account.

TIP

OneDrive provides storage but not a backup (duplicate). If you delete a file from OneDrive, any copies stored on linked computers are also deleted.

In this chapter, you copy files to a flash drive to transport between machines or as an ad hoc backup. You also use the Backup function, which automatically copies files as a backup. Consider this scenario: You write a letter to a friend and save it to your Documents folder. Later that day, you delete part of the letter and save it again, replacing the original document. The next day, you wish you still had the deleted text. The Backup function comes to your rescue because it saves versions of files; you can recover the latest version or an earlier version of a file. As I wrote this book, I saved it hundreds of times — the Backup function could save every version, allowing me to roll back to an earlier copy, to before I had made some big goof. (That's purely hypothetical, of course.)

Finally, in this chapter you explore the Reset function, a tool you may need if you have problems with your computer. The Reset function reinstalls Windows 10 but preserves your personal data.

Add an External Hard Drive or Flash Drive

1. Before you attach a flash drive or hard drive to your computer, consider the following options that Windows 10 automatically offers for using the newly attached disk:

   - **Configure This Drive for Backup** uses the new drive for the File History function and is best suited to large-capacity drives, at least 500GB. See "Turn On File History," later in this chapter.

   - **Configure Storage Settings** opens the Settings app so that you can configure the storage settings on your computer.

   - **Open Folder to View Files** displays the contents of the disk in File Explorer on the desktop. You select this option to copy files to or from the drive you're attaching.

   - **Take No Action** dismisses the notification.

TIP Notifications appear for the amount of time specified in PC Settings. If the notification disappears before you can select it, you can redisplay it by removing and then reinserting the drive or USB cable.

2. Locate an unused USB port on your computer. A *USB port* is a small rectangular slot on the front or back of a desktop computer or along any edge of a laptop or tablet computer. USB ports are often marked with a symbol that looks like a trident, as shown in **Figure 15-1**.

TIP If a USB port is hard to reach, you can buy an extension cable from any office supply store. You can also buy a *hub*, which adds ports to your computer.

3. If you're using a flash drive, insert it into the USB slot. USB fits one way only. If you're using an external hard drive, plug it into a power source, if one is required, and then connect a cable to the USB port. Turn on the external drive, if it has a separate power switch. (Flash drives and some external hard drives don't have separate power supplies or switches.)

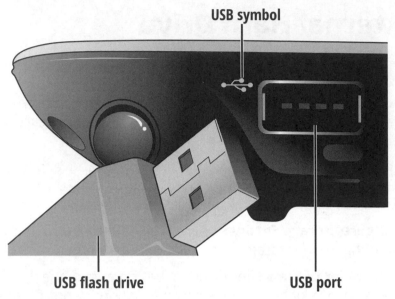

USB symbol

USB flash drive   USB port

FIGURE 15-1

4. Windows 10 displays a notification to *Check to see what happens with removable drives*. (You can click the mouse instead of tapping.) If you select the first notification, a list of choices appears, as shown in **Figure 15-2**. If you know which action you want to take, you can select that action. Otherwise, select Take No Action or wait until the notification disappears on its own.

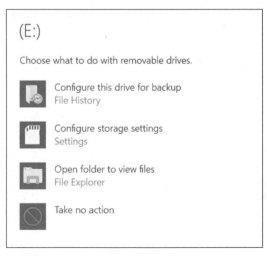

FIGURE 15-2

Copy Files to or from a Flash Drive

1. To copy files or folders to a flash drive, insert the flash drive into one of your computer's USB ports.

TIP

Laptops, like cameras, often have a slot for a memory card. Want to turn your memory card into a flash drive? Simply buy a device called a dedicated or single-purpose memory card reader. Strictly speaking, a multipurpose card reader also works, but multicard readers cost more and are often larger than single-card readers. In addition, a dedicated memory card reader doesn't need a cable to connect a camera to a computer. You can just download your pictures to your hard drive from the card.

2. If Windows 10 displays a notification (refer to **Figure 15-2**) when you insert the flash drive or memory card, select Open Folder to View Files, which will open File Explorer on the desktop. If File Explorer doesn't open automatically, go to the desktop and then select the yellow folder icon in the taskbar to open File Explorer.

TIP

The keyboard shortcut to open File Explorer is ⊞+E.

3. In File Explorer, navigate on the left to the folder that contains the files you want to copy. See Chapter 14 for information on navigating in File Explorer. Select the folder.

4. On the right side of File Explorer, select the folder or file you want to copy. If you see a check box to the left of each object you want to copy, you can select each check box to copy multiple files simultaneously. (If you don't see check boxes next to files, see Chapter 14 for information on enabling this function for file selection.)

TIP

To select every object on the right simultaneously, use the Select All button on the Home tab. You can also select the files you don't want to copy and then use the Invert Selection button on the Home tab; deselected files become selected and vice versa. You can select files in other ways as well.

The keyboard shortcut to select all files in File Explorer is Ctrl+A.

5. In the Ribbon, select the Home tab and then select the Copy To button, as shown in **Figure 15-3**. Select Choose Location from the menu that appears.

TIP

You can move files if you want them gone from their original location. To do so, select the Move To button. Follow the remaining steps, but substitute the word *Move* for *Copy*.

Select the Copy To button

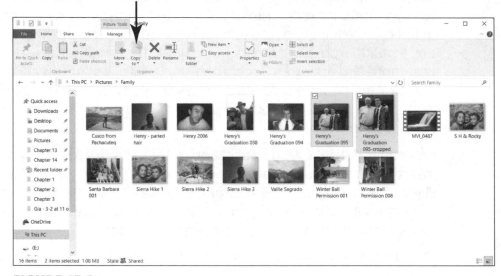

FIGURE 15-3

6. In the Copy Items window, under the This PC heading, locate the flash drive or memory card. The drive will not be Local Disk (C:), where Windows 10 resides. Select the removable flash drive or memory card to which you want to copy the files, as shown in **Figure 15-4,** and then select the Copy button. If the files copy quickly, you may not see any indication of progress; otherwise, a progress bar is displayed until copying is complete.

TIP

If you select your user name in the Copy Items dialog box, you may see OneDrive listed in the expanded list. Files you copy to OneDrive are automatically copied to the cloud and to linked computers.

7. If you copy a file that is already on the destination disk, the Replace or Skip Files window appears, as shown in **Figure 15-5**. (Perhaps you're copying a newer version of a file you copied before.) Note the available options:

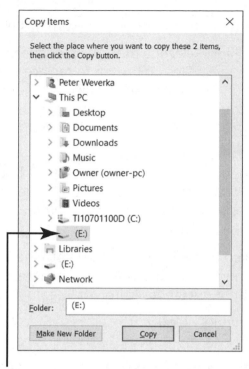

Select a location for the copy

FIGURE 15-4

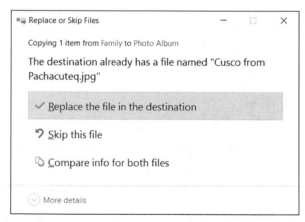

FIGURE 15-5

- **Replace the File in the Destination:** Selecting this option replaces one file with another. Be certain that you don't need the replaced file (as you might if you want to keep different versions of files).

- **Skip This File:** Selecting this option does nothing with this file.

- **Compare Info for Both Files:** Selecting this option opens another window in which you can select files on the left to replace those on the right, and select files on the right to keep. Selecting the same file on the left and right creates a second file with a number added to the name, such as *my file (2).* This option enables you to have the original and the new file.

Select one of the previous options. If you selected Compare Info for Both Files, select the files to replace or skip, and then select the Continue button. You may or may not see a progress indicator, depending on how quickly the files are copied.

8. Confirm that the copy worked by navigating on the left to the location you selected as the destination in Step 6. If the files are there, congratulations; you're done. If not, try Steps 4 through 6 again.

9. Remove the flash drive or memory card you inserted in Step 1. You're good to go.

TIP

If you have files or folders that you'd be devastated to lose, follow the steps in this task to create backup copies of those items on a portable storage device. Then keep that device in a safe place.

TIP

To copy files from a flash drive or memory card, follow these same steps but select the flash drive in Step 3 and the folder or other destination to which you want to copy or move files in Step 6.

Turn On File History

1. To enable Windows 10 to create backup copies of your files, first make sure that an external drive such as a hard drive or flash drive is connected to your computer. Then select the Start button and choose Settings on the Start menu.

2. In the Settings window, select Update & Security. Then select Backup in the Update & Security window. A Back Up Using File History screen opens, as shown in **Figure 15-6**. Which screen you see depends on whether you have told Windows 10 where you want to keep backup copies of your files.

Select More Options to indicate where the backup drive is

Turn on file history

FIGURE 15-6

TIP

Another way to access the Back Up Using File History screen is to select Configure This Drive for Backup when you attach an external hard drive.

TIP

File History stores information on an external drive or a network location. After you turn on File History, it will automatically create copies of your documents and photos on the drive you identify. If you lose, delete, or change your mind about changes to a file, you can restore the backup copy created by File History following the steps in the "Restore Files with File History" section, later in this chapter.

3. If necessary, tell Windows 10 where to keep backup copies of your files. (If your screen looks like **Figure 15-6, bottom**, Windows 10 already recognizes where your backup drive is located; skip to Step 4.) Select the More Options link (shown in **Figure 15-6, top**), and in the Backup Options window, select See Advanced Settings (you'll find it at the bottom of the screen). The File History window opens. It lists the external drives connected to your computer. Select the Turn On button. Then close the Settings app and repeat Steps 1 and 2 to return to the Back Up Using File History screen (shown in **Figure 15-6, bottom**).

4. Turn on the Automatically Back Up My Files setting (shown in **Figure 15-6, bottom**) if this setting isn't already turned on. Windows 10 starts copying files to your hard drive.

5. Select More Options to tell Windows 10 which folders to back up and how often to back up the folders. The Backup Options screen opens, as shown in **Figure 15-7**. By default, Windows 10 saves copies of files every hour, but you can change this and other file history settings, as follows:

   - **Back Up My Files:** This option controls how frequently File History checks for new or changed files. I recommend that you select Every 10 Minutes to minimize the chances of losing new or changed documents.

TIP

   When you go on vacation, consider disconnecting the external drive and storing it in a fireproof safe or a safe deposit box. The drive is your insurance against theft or destruction.

   - **Keep My Backups:** By default, File History keeps copies of your files forever. This option allows you to limit how long copies are kept. Leave this set as Forever.

   - **Back Up These Folders:** File History provides a laundry list of folders to back up.

   To remove a folder, select it in the list. The Remove button appears. Select this button. Folders you remove are added to the Exclude These Folders list at the bottom of the Backup Options screen.

To add a folder, select the Add a Folder button. Then select the folder in the Select Folder dialog box.

- **Back Up to a Different Drive:** Select the Stop Using Drive button and repeat Steps 1 through 3 to choose a different external drive for keeping backup copies of your files.

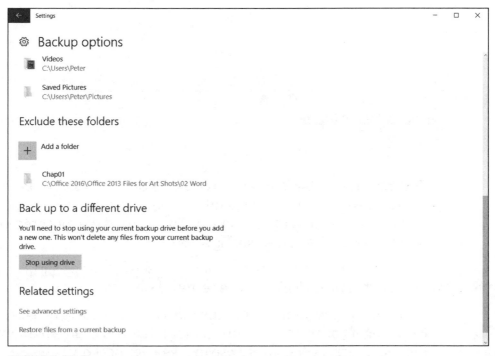

FIGURE 15-7

Restore Files with File History

1. In the Search box on the taskbar, type **file history**. On the search results screen, select Restore Your Files with File History – Control Panel. File History opens on the desktop.

2. Select the Restore Personal Files link. You see a screen similar to the one in **Figure 15-8**.

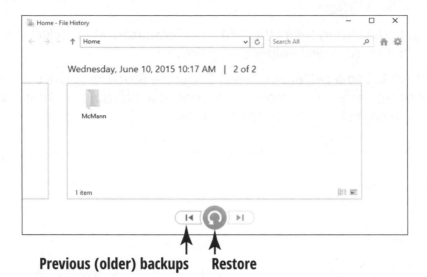

Wednesday, June 10, 2015 10:17 AM | 2 of 2

McMann

1 item

Previous (older) backups   **Restore**

FIGURE 15-8

3. The most recent backup versions created by File History appear in the window. To see other versions of backups, select the left-pointing arrow at the bottom of the window. To return to the most recent backup, select the right-pointing arrow.

TIP

Don't select the Restore button until you select the specific file(s) you want. Otherwise, all files will be restored simultaneously.

TIP

Generally, you want to restore the most recent version of a file. However, if you want to restore content that you changed prior to the most recent version, browse to an earlier backup.

4. If you know the location of the file you want to restore, you can open that location with a double-click or double-tap. If you're not sure of the location, select the search box in the upper-right corner and type the document name. Matching results appear as you type. Select the file you want to restore.

TIP

On a touchscreen, the virtual keyboard doesn't appear on the desktop until you select the keyboard icon on the right side of the taskbar.

5. Select the Restore button. If you restored a file you previously deleted, you can close File History. Skip the remaining steps.

6. If the Replace or Skip Files window opens (refer to **Figure 15-5**) in the preceding step, a version of the file exists in the original location.

If you're sure you want to restore the previous version of the file, you can choose Replace the File in the Destination Folder. However, to see additional options, select Compare Info for Both Files. The File Conflict window appears.

7. In the File Conflict window, consider the following selections:

- Select files on the left to replace files in the destination with the backup files. (This is the same as selecting Replace on the Replace or Skip Files screen.)

- Select files on the right to cancel restoring those files. (This is the same as selecting Skip on the Replace or Skip Files screen.)

- If you select the same files on both sides of the window, File History will leave the original as is and restore the backup version with the same name plus *(2)*, allowing you to have both versions. (You need this option only if you're uncertain about which version you want.)

TIP

If you're restoring multiple files at the same time, you can select different options for each: replace one, skip another, and have File History create a copy for another. That's a lot of choices in one little window.

8. Select Continue, and Windows 10 completes the operation based on your choices in Step 7. The location of the restored files opens in File Explorer.

Reset a Misbehaving Computer

1. Glitch happens. The computer misbehaves, a program crashes, or the machine becomes unexpectedly slow. If your computer is misbehaving, try resetting it. Click the Start button and choose Settings. In the Settings window, select Update & Security. In the Update & Security window, select Recovery.

TIP

Before you reset your PC, see Chapter 12 for information about updating and maintaining Windows 10. Updating Windows may resolve some problems.

The Reset function should leave your data alone and unchanged. However, consider following Steps 1–4 in the section "Restore Files with File History" to confirm that your external drive contains all your files. Better safe than sorry.

2. Under Reset This PC, select the Get Started button, as shown in **Figure 15-9**.

The Reset function doesn't remove apps installed through the Microsoft Store but does remove any apps you installed any other way. This safety feature is based on the assumption that something you installed from some other source is causing a problem. Be certain that you either don't need a desktop app or you have the materials necessary to reinstall a desktop app, such as Microsoft Office. Windows 10 will create a file on the desktop after the fact, identifying the programs it removed.

This is where you want to click

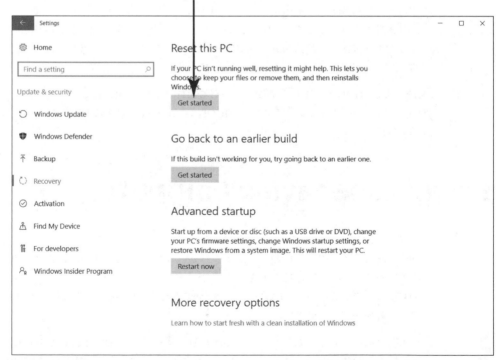

FIGURE 15-9

3. In the Choose an Option dialog box, select Keep My Files. (Or select Cancel, if you're just exploring this feature and don't want to continue with it.)

4. Reset runs, and your computer will restart at least once. When the reset process is complete, the Lock screen appears. Sign in as usual. If you see a file named *Removed Apps* on the desktop, double-click or double-tap it to open that file in your browser. The removed apps are listed. If you're aware that one of these apps created a problem, don't reinstall it.

TIP

Don't be intimidated by the Reset function — it's easy, quick, and worthwhile if it makes a problem computer run better.

Index

About the Author

Peter Weverka is the best-selling author of many *For Dummies* books, including *Office 2013 All-in-One For Dummies*, as well as four dozen other books about various topics. Peter's humorous articles and stories (not related to computers, thankfully) have appeared in *Harper's*, *SPY*, and other magazines for grown-ups.

Author's Acknowledgments

Thanks to Mark Justice Hinton for writing the first edition of this book. Much of Mark's work lives on in this edition. I would also like to thank Amy Fandrei at Wiley for giving me the opportunity to write this book and Colleen Diamond and Susan Christophersen for editing it. Thanks as well go to Russ Mullen, the technical editor, who made sure all instructions were accurate.

Publisher's Acknowledgments

Acquisitions Editor: Amy Fandrei

Project Manager: Colleen Diamond

Development Editor: Colleen Diamond

Copy Editors: Colleen Diamond and Susan Christophersen

Technical Editor: Russ Mullen

Editorial Manager: Mary Corder

Editorial Assistant: Serena Novosel

Sr. Editorial Assistant: Cherie Case

Production Editor: Vasanth Koilraj

Cover Photo: © haveseen/Shutterstock

Apple & Mac

iPad For Dummies,
6th Edition
978-1-118-72306-7

iPhone For Dummies,
7th Edition
978-1-118-69083-3

Macs All-in-One
For Dummies, 4th Edition
978-1-118-82210-4

OS X Mavericks
For Dummies
978-1-118-69188-5

Blogging & Social Media

Facebook For Dummies,
5th Edition
978-1-118-63312-0

Social Media Engagement
For Dummies
978-1-118-53019-1

WordPress For Dummies,
6th Edition
978-1-118-79161-5

Business

Stock Investing
For Dummies, 4th Edition
978-1-118-37678-2

Investing For Dummies,
6th Edition
978-0-470-90545-6

Personal Finance

Personal Finance
For Dummies, 7th Edition
978-1-118-11785-9

QuickBooks 2014
For Dummies
978-1-118-72005-9

Small Business Marketing
Kit For Dummies,
3rd Edition
978-1-118-31183-7

Careers

Job Interviews
For Dummies, 4th Edition
978-1-118-11290-8

Job Searching with Social
Media For Dummies,
2nd Edition
978-1-118-67856-5

Personal Branding
For Dummies
978-1-118-11792-7

Resumes For Dummies,
6th Edition
978-0-470-87361-8

Starting an Etsy Business
For Dummies, 2nd Edition
978-1-118-59024-9

Diet & Nutrition

Belly Fat Diet For Dummies
978-1-118-34585-6

Mediterranean Diet
For Dummies
978-1-118-71525-3

Nutrition For Dummies,
5th Edition
978-0-470-93231-5

Digital Photography

Digital SLR Photography
All-in-One For Dummies,
2nd Edition
978-1-118-59082-9

Digital SLR Video &
Filmmaking For Dummies
978-1-118-36598-4

Photoshop Elements 12
For Dummies
978-1-118-72714-0

Gardening

Herb Gardening
For Dummies, 2nd Edition
978-0-470-61778-6

Gardening with Free-Range
Chickens For Dummies
978-1-118-54754-0

Health

Boosting Your Immunity
For Dummies
978-1-118-40200-9

Diabetes For Dummies,
4th Edition
978-1-118-29447-5

Living Paleo For Dummies
978-1-118-29405-5

Big Data

Big Data For Dummies
978-1-118-50422-2

Data Visualization
For Dummies
978-1-118-50289-1

Hadoop For Dummies
978-1-118-60755-8

Language & Foreign Language

500 Spanish Verbs
For Dummies
978-1-118-02382-2

English Grammar
For Dummies, 2nd Edition
978-0-470-54664-2

French All-in-One
For Dummies
978-1-118-22815-9

German Essentials
For Dummies
978-1-118-18422-6

Italian For Dummies,
2nd Edition
978-1-118-00465-4

e **Available in print and e-book formats.**

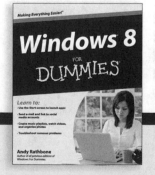

Available wherever books are sold. **For more information or to order direct visit www.dummies.com**

Math & Science

Algebra I For Dummies,
2nd Edition
978-0-470-55964-2

Anatomy and Physiology
For Dummies, 2nd Edition
978-0-470-92326-9

Astronomy For Dummies,
3rd Edition
978-1-118-37697-3

Biology For Dummies,
2nd Edition
978-0-470-59875-7

Chemistry For Dummies,
2nd Edition
978-1-118-00730-3

1001 Algebra II Practice
Problems For Dummies
978-1-118-44662-1

Microsoft Office

Excel 2013 For Dummies
978-1-118-51012-4

Office 2013 All-in-One
For Dummies
978-1-118-51636-2

PowerPoint 2013
For Dummies
978-1-118-50253-2

Word 2013 For Dummies
978-1-118-49123-2

Music

Blues Harmonica
For Dummies
978-1-118-25269-7

Guitar For Dummies,
3rd Edition
978-1-118-11554-1

iPod & iTunes
For Dummies, 10th Edition
978-1-118-50864-0

Programming

Beginning Programming
with C For Dummies
978-1-118-73763-7

Excel VBA Programming
For Dummies, 3rd Edition
978-1-118-49037-2

Java For Dummies,
6th Edition
978-1-118-40780-6

Religion & Inspiration

The Bible For Dummies
978-0-7645-5296-0

Buddhism For Dummies,
2nd Edition
978-1-118-02379-2

Catholicism For Dummies,
2nd Edition
978-1-118-07778-8

Self-Help & Relationships

Beating Sugar Addiction
For Dummies
978-1-118-54645-1

Meditation For Dummies,
3rd Edition
978-1-118-29144-3

Seniors

Laptops For Seniors
For Dummies, 3rd Edition
978-1-118-71105-7

Computers For Seniors
For Dummies, 3rd Edition
978-1-118-11553-4

iPad For Seniors
For Dummies, 6th Edition
978-1-118-72826-0

Social Security
For Dummies
978-1-118-20573-0

Smartphones & Tablets

Android Phones
For Dummies, 2nd Edition
978-1-118-72030-1

Nexus Tablets
For Dummies
978-1-118-77243-0

Samsung Galaxy S 4
For Dummies
978-1-118-64222-1

Samsung Galaxy Tabs
For Dummies
978-1-118-77294-2

Test Prep

ACT For Dummies,
5th Edition
978-1-118-01259-8

ASVAB For Dummies,
3rd Edition
978-0-470-63760-9

GRE For Dummies,
7th Edition
978-0-470-88921-3

Officer Candidate Tests
For Dummies
978-0-470-59876-4

Physician's Assistant Exam
For Dummies
978-1-118-11556-5

Series 7 Exam For Dummies
978-0-470-09932-2

Windows 8

Windows 8.1 All-in-One
For Dummies
978-1-118-82087-2

Windows 8.1 For Dummies
978-1-118-82121-3

Windows 8.1 For Dummies,
Book + DVD Bundle
978-1-118-82107-7

Available in print and e-book formats.

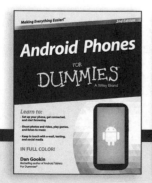

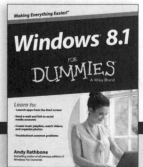

Available wherever books are sold. **For more information or to order direct visit www.dummies.com**

Take Dummies with you everywhere you go!

Whether you are excited about e-books, want more from the web, must have your mobile apps, or are swept up in social media, Dummies makes everything easier.

Leverage the Power

For Dummies is the global leader in the reference category and one of the most trusted and highly regarded brands in the world. No longer just focused on books, customers now have access to the For Dummies content they need in the format they want. Let us help you develop a solution that will fit your brand and help you connect with your customers.

Advertising & Sponsorships

Connect with an engaged audience on a powerful multimedia site, and position your message alongside expert how-to content.

Targeted ads • Video • Email marketing • Microsites • Sweepstakes sponsorship

21 Million Monthly Page Views & 13 Million Unique Visitors

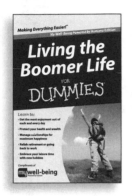

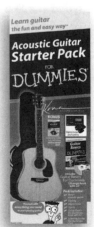